Macmillan English

Language Book

DIGITAL EDITION AVAILABLE

Mary Bowen
Printha Ellis
Louis Fidge

D1260113

macmillan
education

Scope and sequence: Units 1-9

	FLUENCY BOOK 1	LANGUAGE BOOK 1		
		Reading and understanding	Working with words	Sentence building
		REVISION		
Unit 1	The island of adventure	reading text: *My family and me* text type: autobiography vocabulary: family	family members	sentences – capital letters and full stops
Unit 2	Sam's house	reading text: *A new room for Amy* text type: descriptive text and poem vocabulary: toys and furniture	furniture toys	common nouns
Unit 3	The moon and the stars	reading text: *Can the moon see me?* text type: poem (x2) vocabulary: night sky	the night sky and creatures	*a* and *an*
		REVISION: UNITS 1-3		
Unit 4	Sam's garden	reading text: *My secret garden* text type: information text vocabulary: animals and colours	colours	sentences – questions
Unit 5	Sam's island	reading text: *Where is my house?* text type: puzzle poem vocabulary: numbers; prepositions	numbers	adjectives – colour words
Unit 6	On the beach	reading text: *We love the beach* text type: story with familiar setting vocabulary: seaside words	marine features and creatures	proper nouns – people's names
		REVISION: UNITS 4-6		
Unit 7	In the jungle	reading text: *Do or don't?* text type: information text vocabulary: action verbs	action verbs	verbs – imperatives
Unit 8	Monkey fun	reading text: *Where are the animals?* text type: information text vocabulary: animals; colours; actions	animals	sentences – statements and questions
Unit 9	In the cave	reading text: *Playtime* text type: descriptive text and traditional rhymes vocabulary: action verbs	more action verbs	verbs – is/are with -ing
		REVISION: UNITS 7-9		

Grammar	Listening	Phonics	Class writing
REVISION			
Hi/Hello. What is your name? I am Tilly. How old are you? I am six.	Who is speaking? (identifying family members)	CVC words with a short **a**	My friends and I (simple sentences)
This is my bed. These are my books. Is this your radio? Yes, it is. / No, it isn't.	Draw the toys (listening for detail)	CVC words with a short **e**	My room (simple description)
I can see a plane. I can't hear an owl. Can you see the moon? Yes, I can. / No, I can't.	What can you hear? (identifying sounds)	CVC words with a short **i**	What can we see? (simple sentences)
REVISION: UNITS 1-3			
What is this? It is a nest. What are these? They are small blue eggs.	What are the animals? (identifying sounds)	CVC words with a short **u**	Animals (questions and answers)
Where is the mouse? It is in / on / under / next to the table.	Complete the picture (listening for location)	CVC words with a short **o**	Where is it? (writing about location)
I have got a starfish. Have you got a starfish? Yes, I have. / No, I haven't. Has he got a rock? Yes, he has. / No, he hasn't.	What has she got? (listening for detail)	words beginning or ending with the **sh** phoneme	What have they got? (describing possessions)
REVISION: UNITS 4-6			
Listen! Please sit down! Don't run! Don't look behind you!	*Simon Says* (understanding commands)	words beginning or ending with the **ch** phoneme	Crossing the road (writing commands)
Look at the parrot. It is sitting in the tree. He is running. They are playing football.	What are they doing? (identifying activities)	words ending with the **ll** phoneme	What are they doing? (1) (writing about activities)
Is he riding a horse? Yes, he is. / No, he isn't. Are they dancing? Yes, they are. / No, they aren't.	*Two Little Hands* (following a sequence of actions)	words ending with the **ng** phoneme	What are they doing? (2) (questions and answers)
REVISION: UNITS 7-9			

Scope and sequence: Units 10-18

	FLUENCY BOOK 1	LANGUAGE BOOK 1		
		Reading and understanding	**Working with words**	**Sentence building**
Unit **10**	In the tree house	reading text: *Suki's day* text type: story with familiar setting vocabulary: times; feelings	feelings	proper nouns – days of the week
Unit **11**	Look at that ship!	reading text: *Here comes the train!* text type: information text vocabulary: action verbs	matching verbs and nouns	pronouns
Unit **12**	On the ship	reading text: *We all love the mall* text type: descriptive text vocabulary: shops	shops	prepositions
		REVISION: UNITS 10-12		
Unit **13**	A hundred steps	reading text: *Dani can count!* text type: story with patterned language vocabulary: numbers	numbers 1-100	verbs – to have
Unit **14**	The weather man	reading text: *Splish, splash, splosh!* text type: story with familiar setting vocabulary: weather	weather	adjectives and nouns
Unit **15**	A ride on an elephant	reading text: *Animal puzzles* text type: puzzle text vocabulary: body parts	parts of the body and physical features	verbs – to be
		REVISION: UNITS 13-15		
Unit **16**	A picnic by the river	reading text: *Let's have a picnic* text type: poem (rap) vocabulary: food	food and drink	nouns – singular and plural with s
Unit **17**	Time to go home	reading text: *At the airport* text type: information text vocabulary: vehicles; clothes; colours	clothing	sentences – word order
Unit **18**	Fireworks!	reading text: *Fireworks!* text type: shape poems vocabulary: fireworks; colours	a word game	verbs – to like
		REVISION: UNITS 16-18		

Grammar	Listening	Phonics	Class writing
It is Saturday. What is the time? It is nine o'clock. It is half past three.	Harry's week (matching days and activities)	words ending with the **ck** phoneme	Days of the week (writing about days, times and locations)
What is he doing? He is eating an ice cream. What are they doing? They are swimming.	People are getting off the train. (locating items in a picture)	words beginning with blends **br cr dr gr** or **tr**	Activities (writing questions and answers)
There is a ball under the chair. There are toys in the box.	Where are they? (identifying locations)	words beginning with blends **bl cl fl** or **pl**	The park (description)
REVISION: UNITS 10-12			
How many trees are there? There are two trees.	How many are there? (listening for detail)	words beginning or ending with the **th** phoneme	Our classroom (description including numbers)
What is the weather like? It is raining / snowing / cold / hot / sunny. Is it cold? Yes, it is. / No, it isn't.	What's the weather like? (identifying weather types)	words beginning with blends **st sm sw sp** or **sn**	The weather (completing a weather diary)
They have got long ears. We have got little ears. We have not got long ears.	What are the animals? (identifying animals)	words ending with the blends **nd nt** or **nk**	Animals (describing animals)
REVISION: UNITS 13-15			
I like grapes. He likes sandwiches. She likes cakes.	Mobi likes everything! (identifying preferences)	words with the spelling pattern **a_e** or **i_e**	Favourite food (writing about food preferences)
Whose hat is this? It is Tilly's. Whose socks are these? They are Sam's.	Whose voice is this? (identifying people)	words with the spelling pattern **ue u_e** or **o_e**	What are they packing? (writing about clothes)
The bird is going onto/over/along the roof. The children are going round / towards / into the house.	What's your favourite? (identifying descriptions)	words ending with the blends **ld lk lp** or **lt**	At the fun fair (description)
REVISION: UNITS 16-18			

5

Hello!

Aa apple   **Bb** bird   **Cc** cat   **Dd** dog   **Ee** elephant   **Ff** frog   **Gg** girl

1 Listen and sing the alphabet song.

2 Listen and point.

3 Now talk to your friend.

Hello, I am …

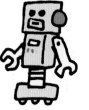

Nn nut   **Oo** orange   **Pp** parrot   **Qq** question   **Rr** robot   **Ss** sun   **Tt** train

Hh Ii Jj Kk Ll Mm

hat   insect   jug   kite   lollipop   monkey

4 **Listen, point and say.** 🎧

5 **Listen and sing.** 🎧

A rainbow, a rainbow,
It's purple and blue.
It's green and yellow,
It's red and orange too.

6 **Point and say.**

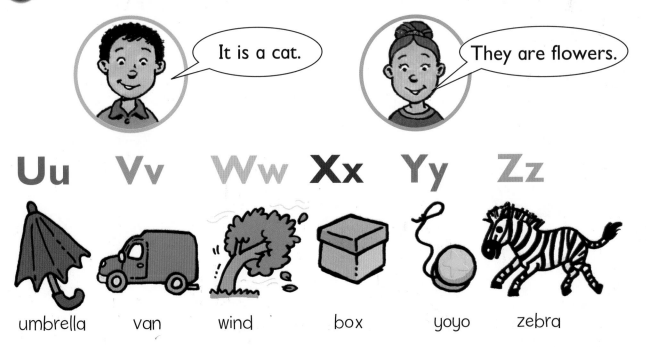

It is a cat.

They are flowers.

Uu Vv Ww Xx Yy Zz

umbrella   van   wind   box   yoyo   zebra

In the classroom

big

little

1 2

1 **Listen and point.** 🎧

Hello, Nina. How are you?

I am fine, thank you. And you?

Fine, thank you.

2 **Now ask and answer.**

| 3 | 4 | 5 | 6 | 7 | 8 | 9 | 10 |

3 **Listen and sing.** 🎧

1, 2, 3, 4, 5,
6, 7, 8, 9, 10.
Stand up!
Clap, clap, clap.

Point to the window,
Point to the door,
Point to the ceiling,
Point to the floor.

1, 2, 3, 4, 5,
6, 7, 8, 9, 10.
Stand up!
Clap, clap, clap.

4 **Listen and do.** 🎧

5 **Listen, point and say.** 🎧

6 **Listen and point.** 🎧

7 **Ask and answer.**

Point to the door.
What colour is it?

Point to the desks.
How many?

My family and me

Hi! I am Tim. I am six. Meet my family.

This is my big brother.
He is ten ...
... and this is me.

This is my dad.
He is really tall ...
... and this is me.

Parents: *see extra material on page 166*

This is my mum.
She is very helpful ...
... and this is me.

This is my sister.
She is funny ...
... and this is me.

This is my baby brother.
He is little ...
... and this is me.

And this is my grandma and my
grandpa. They are very kind ...
... and this is me.

These are my friends and
this is my teacher ...
... and this is me.

This is my pet dog, Jack.
He is a lot of fun ...
... and this is me.

Reading and understanding

1 **Look and read. Then choose and circle.**

1 This is Tim's   brother.
                  sister.

2 This is Tim's   mother.
                  father.

3 This is Tim's   friend.
                  teacher.

2 **Choose the word from the box.**

tall   kind   funny   helpful

You can also say **very** before these words.

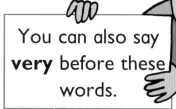

1 Tim's father is ──────── .

2 Tim's mother is ──────── .

3 Tim's grandmother and grandfather are ──────── .

4 Tim's sister is ──────── .

Working with words

1 **Write the words.**

sister	mum	grandma
grandpa	dad	brother

1

My _____ is big.

2

My _____ is kind.

3

My _____ is kind, too.

4

My _____ is funny.

5

My _____ is tall.

6

My _____ is helpful.

Sentence building

A B C D E F G H I J K L M N O P Q R S T U V W X Y Z

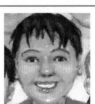

A sentence begins with a **capital letter**.

A sentence ends with a **full stop**.

My brother is ten**.**

1 **Read the sentences. Circle the capital letters and full stops.**
1   Tim is six.
2   This is my sister.
3   Jack is my pet dog.
4   My mum is helpful.
5   My grandma and grandpa are kind.

Grammar

Look at this!

I am Tilly. I am six.

Sam is my friend. He is eight.

Nina is my friend. She is seven.

Tilly

Sam

Nina

1 Point and say.

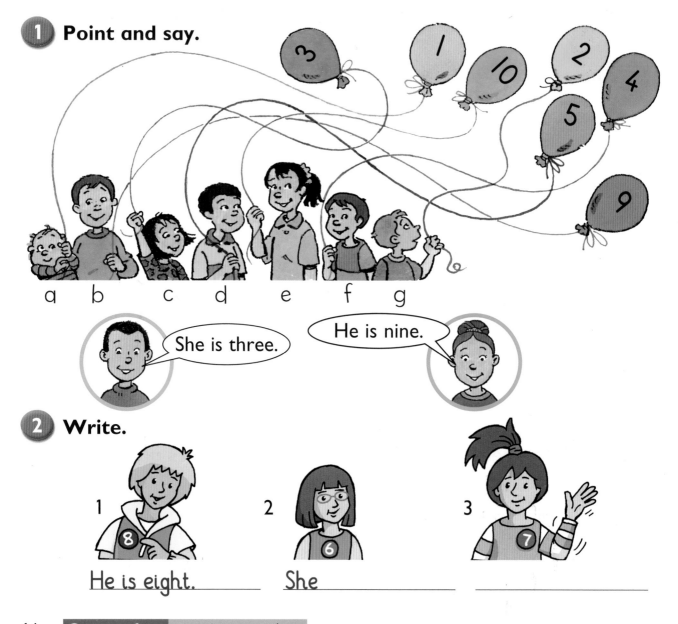

a b c d e f g

She is three.

He is nine.

2 Write.

1 He is eight.

2 She _____

3 _____

Grammar focus expressing name and age

Listening

This is my family.

Nina

1 **Listen to Nina and her family. Tick ✓ the box.** 🎧

1 dad	☐	mum	☐
2 sister	☐	brother	☐
3 grandma	☐	grandpa	☐
4 dad	☐	brother	☐
5 grandma	☐	sister	☐
6 grandpa	☐	mum	☐

2 **Listen and sing.** 🎧

Father, mother, sister, brother,
Sister, brother, father, mother,
Father, sister, mother, brother,
And me.

Phonics

1 **Listen and read.** 🎧

Sam has got a **c**a**t**.

The **c**a**t** is on the m**a**t.

The **c**a**t** has got a h**a**t.

Ca**n** you see the **c**a**t**?

2 **Say the sounds. Make the words.**

1

2

3

| c | a | t |

| m | a | t |

| h | a | t |

_____cat_____

_____

_____

3 **Write.**

1 _____ has got a _____ .

2 The _____ is on the _____ .

4 **Tick ✓ the words you can read.**

Sam ☐   cat ☐   hat ☐   mat ☐

Class writing

Write about Nina and her friend.
Write in the bubbles.

Hi!
I am Nina.
I am seven.
Sam is my friend.
He is eight.

Remember!
I **am** …
He **is** …
She **is** …

1

2

3

4

A new room for Amy

Parents: see extra material on page 166

This is my new bed.

And this is my little table.

This is my big desk.

And here is the chair.

This is my computer. It is pink!

These are my books. I like story books.

And this is my radio.

This is my toy box
and these are my toys.

And these are my 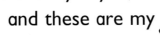 elephants!

I love elephants.

Even my lamp is an elephant!

Toys

A doll and a train,

A plane and a ball,

These are my toys

And I love them all.

Reading and understanding

1 **Read and circle answer A or B.**

A   B

1 This is Amy's new baby sister.

2 This is Amy's computer. It is pink.

3 This is Amy's big desk.

4 These are Amy's elephants.

5 This is Amy's lamp.

Remember!
This **is** a desk. These **are** desk**s**.

2 **Arrange this poem. Write the numbers. Read the poem.**

☐ These are my toys

☐ A plane and a ball,

☐ And I love them all.

1 A doll and a train,

Get active 2

Working with words

1 **Find the words.**

1   2   3  4   5   6

balldeskchairdolltableplane

2 **Write the words in the toy box or the bedroom.**

ball

Sentence building

A **noun** is a naming word.

ball   doll   table

1 **Match the picture and the noun.**

1 bed ☐   2 radio ☐   3 train ☐   4 plane ☐   5 lamp ☐

a    b    c    d   e

Grammar

Look at this!

These are toys.

This is a bed.

This is a table.

These are books.

1 **Say and then write.**

a computer   a ball   chairs   books

1 This is _____ .

2 These are _____ .

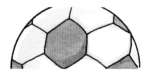

3 These are _____ .

4 This is _____ .

2 **Complete the sentences.**

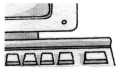

1 _____ elephants.

2 _____ a doll.

3 **What are they? Look and say.**

1   2    3   4

5   6   7   8

This is …

These are …

Grammar focus   *use of* this is *and* these are

Listening

2

These are my toys.

1 **Listen and match.** 🎧

1 ☐   2 ☐   3 ☐   4 ☐   5 ☐   6 ☐

a   b   c   d   e   f

2 **Talk about the children and their toys.**

This is Tilly. These are her dolls.

3 **Listen and say.** 🎧

Hi! I am Ben and this is my dog.

This is Sam and this is his frog.

This is Tilly and this is her cat. A cat in a hat and a frog and a dog, and that's that!

Phonics

1 **Listen and read.**

 Ben has got a hen. The hen is red.

Ben has got a pen. The pen is red.

 Ben has got a bed. The bed is red.

2 **Say the sounds. Make the words.**

1    2   3

| B | e | n | | p | e | n | | h | e | n |

_____   _____   _____

3 **Write.**

1    2

Here is _____ in   _____ has got a

a _____ _____ .   a _____ _____ .

4 **Tick ✓ the words you can read.**

Ben ☐   hen ☐   pen ☐   bed ☐   red ☐

Class writing

Let's write about things in a room.

1 Listen and colour.

1

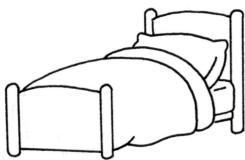

This is a bed. It is blue.

2

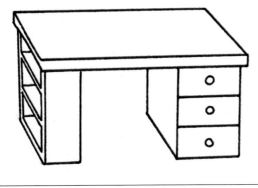

3

4

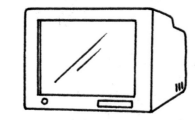

5

Don't forget!
This is a bed.
It is blue.

2 Now write.

Can the moon see me?

I can see the moon
Shining in the sea.
I can see the moon
But can the moon see me?

Oh, shining moon
In shining sea,
Oh, Mr Moon,
Please look at me!

I can hear an owl
Tu-whooing in a tree.
I can hear an owl
But can the owl hear me?

Tu-whit, tu-whoo,
Tu-whoo, tu-whee.
I can hear the owl.
Can it hear me?

Parents: see extra material on page 166

Star light, Star bright,
First star I see tonight.
I wish I may, I wish I might
Have the wish I wish tonight.

Reading and understanding

1 **Ask and answer.**

Yes   No   I don't know

Can you see the moon?
Can you see the sea?
Can you hear the moon?
Can the moon see you?
Can you see an owl?
Can you hear an owl?
Can the owl see you?
Can the owl hear you?

2 **Read and circle the rhyming words.**

Star light, Star bright,
First star I see tonight.
I wish I may, I wish I might
Have the wish I wish tonight.

Remember!
sea rhymes with **me**
bright rhymes with **might**

3 **Read the words. Point to the picture and say. Then colour.**

moon   sea   island
tree   star

I can see a star.

Get active 3

Comprehension focus   consolidation of new language and understanding of rhyme

Working with words

1 **Trace the words.**

star moon owl tree

Sentence building

We say **an** with words which begin with **a**, **e**, **i**, **o** or **u**.

an apple   an egg   an ice cream   an orange   an umbrella

We say **a** with all other words.

a star   a bed   a tree

1 **Say *a* or *an*.**

1 _____ bird    2 _____ owl

3 _____ elephant   4 _____ plane

5 _____ desk    6 _____ balloon

2 **Write *a* or *an*.**

1 **Ask and answer.**

the sun owl tree the moon a star a bird

2 **Look at the big picture above and say. Then write.**

1

I can see the ——————.

I can't see the ——————.

2

I can see a ——————.

I can't see a ——————.

3 **Look at the big picture and write.**

I ——————— a bird.   I ——————— an owl.

Listening

1 **Listen and point.**

2 **Listen again and circle the pictures.**

3 **Now listen and say.**

I can hear an owl.

4 **Listen and sing.**

Twinkle, twinkle, little star,
How I wonder what you are,
Up above the world so high,
Like a diamond in the sky.
Twinkle, twinkle, little star,
How I wonder what you are.

Phonics

1 **Listen and read**

This is my w**i**g. My w**i**g is b**i**g.

This is my t**i**n. My t**i**n is b**i**g.

This is my b**i**n. My b**i**n is b**i**g.

My b**i**g t**i**n is **i**n my b**i**g b**i**n.

2 **Say the sounds. Make the words.**

1

2

3

   b **i** n

   t **i** n

w **i** g

3 **Write.**

1

2

3

This is a ———— .   This is my ———— .   This is ———— .

4 **Tick ✓ the words you can read.**

| bin ☐ | tin ☐ | big ☐ | wig ☐ |

Phonics focus *words with a short* **i** *sound*

Class writing

Let's write about what we can see.

1 **Find and colour.**

Can you see… ?

a car   a train   a plane   a dog   a cat   a mouse

2 **Write.**

I can see a plane. I can see _____

_____

_____

Revision 1

You can do it!

1 Look at the pictures. What can you see?

2 Listen and read.

3 Read and say.
Look at picture 1:
What can Sam hear?
Can he see it?

Look at picture 2:
Where is Sam's mobile?
Can Nina see it?
Can she hear it?

Look at pictures 3 and 4:
Can you see Sam's mobile?
What can you see?

Look at picture 5:
Is this Sam's mobile?

1 The children are in Sam's tree house.

2 Ben can hear the mobile. It is in a big box.

Listen! It's in this box.

Yes! I can hear it.

4 Is this your mobile?

No. These are my sunglasses.

6 I can _____ but I can't _____.

Hello, _____.

Hi, _____.

4 Listen, point and say which picture.

5 Finish the story.
Look at picture 6.
His name is Mobi.
What is her name?

6 Act out the story.

7 Listen and say the chant.

This is a cat.
This is a hat.
This is a fat cat in a hat.
Miaow.

This is a hen.
This is a nest.
This is a red hen in a nest.
Cluck, cluck.

My secret garden

This is my garden.
Here is the key.
Open the door,
And what can we see?

a beautiful yellow
butterfly

a long brown snake
in the tall grass

Parents: see extra material on page 166

purple flowers
on the wall

a nest with three
small blue eggs

red apples
on a tree

an orange goldfish
in a pond

a green frog on a rock

a big black beetle

Reading and understanding

1 **Read and colour. Match and say.**

1 an orange goldfish on a tree ▢

2 a green frog on the wall  ▢

3 red apples in the pond ▢

4 a long brown snake on a rock ▢

5 three small blue eggs in a nest ▢

6 purple flowers in the tall grass ▢

Remember! in  on

2 **Choose the words. Read the sentences.**

| beautiful | small | long | tall |

1 The grass is _____. 2 The butterfly is _____.

3 The eggs are _____. 4 The snake is _____.

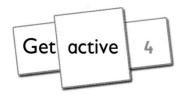

Comprehension focus *consolidation of new language in* My Secret Garden

4

Working with words

1 **Write the words in the correct box.**

| brown purple butterfly green goldfish orange beetle |

colours	**animals**
brown	

2 **Write the name of something from the story under each colour.**

blue	red	orange	brown

Sentence building

Look at this sentence. It is a question.

*A sentence begins with a **capital letter**.*

 What is this?

*This sentence ends with a **question mark**.*

1 **Read the sentences. Circle the capital letters.**

1 W h a t   i s   t h i s ?
2 W h a t   a r e   t h e s e ?
3 I s   t h e   f r o g   g r e e n ?
4 A r e   t h e   f l o w e r s   p u r p l e ?
5 I s   t h e   s n a k e   i n   t h e   t a l l   g r a s s ?

2 **Now circle the question marks.**

Grammar

Look at this!

What is this?

It is a nest.

What are these?

They are eggs.

1 **What is this? Point and say.**

What is this?

It is a bird.

1  2

3  4

2 **What are these? Point and say.**

What are these?

They are bees.

1  2

3  4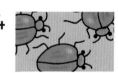

3 **Now write.**

1 What ——————— ? ——————— a flower.

2 What ——————— ? ———————

3 What ——————— ? ———————

4 What ——————— ? ———————

40   **Grammar focus**   What is this? / What are these?; It is … / They are …

Listening

What is this?

: ☐

a bird ☐

☐

dogs ☐

☐

cats ☐

☐

a mouse ☐

ck. 🎧

t goes like this and that.
big and terribly fat.
ngers
bes
gracious -
!

Phonics

1 **Listen and read.**

Run, sun! Run after the bun!
Run, run, run, sun and bun.

Run, jug! Run after the mug!
Run, run, run, jug and mug.

2 **Say the sounds. Make the words.**

1 s u n

2 b u n

3 r u n

4 m u g

5 j u g

3 **Write.**

1 Sam can _____ in the _____.

2 Sam has got a _____ and a _____.

4 **Tick ✓ the words you can read.**

bun ☐ run ☐ sun ☐ jug ☐ mug ☐

Phonics focus *words with a short **u** sound*

Class writing

 Let's write about animals.

cat   elephant   mouse   frog   monkey   bird

1 Draw the animals.

1 What is this?

It is an _____

2 What are these?

They are _____

3 What is this?

_____

4 What are these?

_____

5 What is this?

_____

6 What are these?

_____

2 Write the answers.

> **Don't forget!**
> What is … ?   What are … ?
> It is a …   They are …

Writing focus   It is … / They are … *statements*

Where is my house?

This is my street.
It isn't very long, but it's beautiful.
Look at all the children!
You can see twelve houses on my street.
Where is my house?

 Parents: *see extra material on page 166*

It isn't next to number three.
It isn't under the big green tree.
It isn't pink and it isn't blue.
It isn't next to number two.
It isn't next to number eight.
It isn't the house with a yellow gate.
It's between ten and twelve
And opposite seven.
Do you know where it is?
It's number eleven!

Reading and understanding

1 **Read and say. Then write the house numbers.**

1 It is between one and three. ☐   2 It is between four and six. ☐

3 It is next to seven. ☐   4 It is opposite six. ☐

5 It is under the tree. ☐   6 It is next to twelve. ☐

2 **Read and choose.**

1  The dog is / is not under the car.

2 The cat is / is not next to the tree.

3  The mouse is / is not between the cats.

4 The girl is / is not in the house.

5 He is / is not opposite the gate.

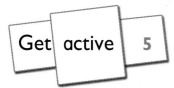 Get active 5

Comprehension focus *consolidation of new language in* Where is my house?

Working with words

1 **Trace and match.**

eleven   three   four

4 **11**   **8** **3**   **12** **7**

seven   eight   twelve

2 **Write these numbers.**

1 _____   2 _____   5 _____

6 _____   9 _____   10 _____

Sentence building

An **adjective** is a describing word.
It tells us more about a noun.

Colour words are adjectives.

a red ball   a blue flower   a brown snake

1 **Read the sentences. Circle the adjectives in red.**

1 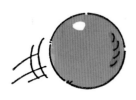 This is a red plane.   2 This is a grey mouse.

3 Here is a green bird.   4 These are brown eggs.

2 **Underline the nouns in blue.**

Grammar

Look at this!

1 Write *Yes* or *No*.

1 The red mouse is in the car. _____

2 The blue mouse is under the table. _____

3 The grey mouse is next to the parrot. _____

4 The orange mouse is between the books. _____

5 The green mouse is on the TV. _____

6 The purple mouse is on the chair. _____

2 Ask and answer.

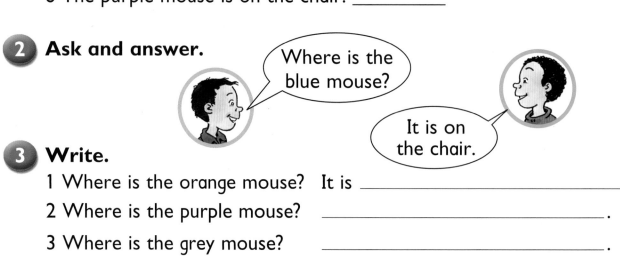

Where is the blue mouse?

It is on the chair.

3 Write.

1 Where is the orange mouse?   It is _____.

2 Where is the purple mouse?   _____.

3 Where is the grey mouse?   _____.

4 Where is the red mouse?   _____.

Grammar focus   *use of prepositions of place*

Listening

Where is the girl?

1 Listen and draw.

2 Ask and answer.

 Where is the girl?

 She is in the sea.

3 Listen and sing. 🎧

Clap, clap hands, one, two, three.
Put your hands upon your knees.
Lift them high to touch the sky.
Clap, clap hands and away they fly.

Phonics

1 **Listen and read.** 🎧

a d**o**g on a l**o**g   a d**o**g in the f**o**g   a d**o**g on a l**o**g in the f**o**g

a f**o**x in a b**o**x   a f**o**x in the f**o**g   a f**o**x in a b**o**x in the f**o**g

2 **Say the sounds. Make the words.**   d   f   l   b

l | og   og   og   ox   ox

<u>log</u>   _____   _____   _____   _____

3 **Write.**

1   Sam is on.
        a _____.

2   This is a _____
        in a _____.

4 **Tick ✓ the words you can read.**

dog ☐   fog ☐   log ☐   box ☐   fox ☐

Class writing

Let's write about where things are.

1 **Talk about the picture. Point and say.**

Number one is in the jungle.

in   on   under   next to   opposite   between

2 **Now write about these houses.**

<u>Number one is</u> _____

_____

_____

_____

_____

We love the beach

It is a beautiful day on the beach. The sky is blue and the sea is green.

Mikey is in the water. 'Wow,' he says. 'I have got a crab!' It is a big red crab.

'Come here,' says his sister, Pat. 'Here is a rock pool. I can see a starfish. It is a baby starfish!'

Grandma has got some shells. 'Listen,' she says. 'You can hear the sea.'

'And I have got some rocks,' says Grandpa. 'Look at all the colours.'

'The pink one is very nice,' says Grandma.

'Yes, it is,' says Grandpa.

Mum and Dad are in their beach chairs. Dad has got a funny hat. Mum has got an umbrella. It is very hot.

'Oh, good! I have got the picnic basket,' says Dad.

'And look!' says Grandpa. 'That man has got ice creams.'

Reading and understanding

1 These sentences from the story are not true.
Say them correctly.

1 The sea is blue.
2 Mum and Dad have got hats.
3 It is not very hot.
4 Mikey's crab is brown.
5 Mikey is next to a rock pool.
6 The starfish is big.
7 Grandpa has got some shells.
8 Pat has got a starfish.

2 Read and circle *Yes* or *No*.

1 Has he got an ice cream?  Yes. No.

2 Has he got a fish?  Yes. No.

3 Has she got a book?  Yes. No.

4 Has she got a basket?  Yes. No.

5 Has he got a cap?  Yes. No.

Get active 6

Working with words

1 **Find the words.**

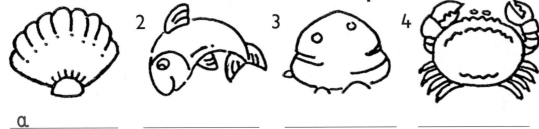

1 bcra 2 ishf 3 lehls 4 rcok

2 **Colour and write the words under the pictures.**

1   2   3   4

a _____   _____   _____   _____

Sentence building

A noun is a naming word.
The name of a person is a **proper noun**.

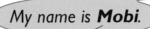

My name is **Mobi**.

A **proper noun** begins with a capital letter.

1 **Write the proper nouns.**

1  2   3

_____   _____   _____

Remember the capital letters.

4 _____ 5   6

_____   _____   _____

Grammar

Look at this!

Look, I have got a starfish.

Look at Sam! He has got a crab.

Look at Nina! She has got a turtle.

1 **Point and say.**

He has got a rock.

She has got a starfish.

2 **Point, ask and answer.**

Has he got a rock?

Has she got a crab?

Yes, he has.

No, she hasn't.

3 **What pets have they got?**

Woof!

Miaow!

1 <u>He_____</u>   2 <u>She_____</u>

Grammar focus   statements and questions with have got

Listening

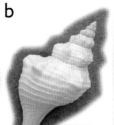

She has got a pink shell.

1 **Listen and tick** ✓.

a   b   c   d

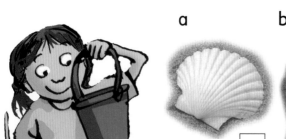 

☐   ☐   ☐   ☐

e   f   g   h

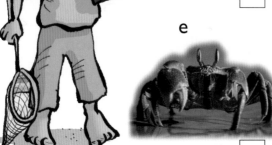  

☐   ☐   ☐   ☐

2 **Point and say.**

She has got a little green crab.

She hasn't got a brown crab.

3 **Listen and sing.**

A sailor went to sea, sea, sea
To see what he could see, see, see.
But all that he could see, see, see
Was the bottom of the deep blue sea, sea, sea.

Phonics

1 **Listen and read.**

This is the **sh**op.

There is a **sh**ip in the **sh**op.

There is a fi**sh** in the **sh**op.

There is a di**sh** in the **sh**op.

2 **Say the sounds. Make the words.**

1   2   3   4

| sh | o | p | sh | i | p | d | i | sh | f | i | sh |

_____   _____   _____   _____

3 **Write.**

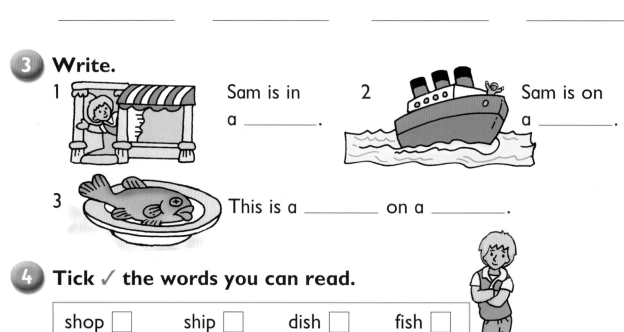

1 Sam is in a _____ .

2 Sam is on a _____ .

3 This is a _____ on a _____ .

4 **Tick ✓ the words you can read.**

| shop ☐ | ship ☐ | dish ☐ | fish ☐ |

Phonics focus   *words with the sh sound and spelling*

Class writing

Let's write about what people have got.

1 **Draw, colour and say.**

She has got a fish. It's blue.

She has got a fish.

It is blue.

2 **Now write.**

Remember!
It's = It is...

Revision 2
You can do it!

1 Look at the pictures. What can you see?

2 Listen and read.

3 Read and say.
Look at picture 1:
Who has got a birthday?
How many cards and presents are there?

Look at picture 2:
What is Tilly and Nina's present?
What has it got?
Does Sam like it?

Look at picture 3:
What is Ben's present?
What colour is it?
How many has Sam got?

Look at picture 4:
What can you see on the table?
What can you see under the table?

Look at pictures 5 and 6:
Who can you see?
What is in the box?
What is the present?
Can you sing it?

1 Today is Sam's birthday. Sam has got cards and presents from his friends.

3 Sam has got a new ball from Ben.

5 What's in the box? Can you guess?

2 Sam has got a lovely book from Nina and Tilly.

What's this? Oh! It's a book. Thank you.

Yes, it's a story book.

Has it got pictures?

Yes, it has.

4 The birthday cake is on the table. One more present is under the table. Who is it from?

Where is the cake?

It's on the table.

6 Mobi is in the box!

Surprise! My present is a song!

Happy birthday to you. Happy birthday to you. Happy birthday, dear Sam. Happy birthday to you.

4 Listen and say. What comes next?

5 Act out Sam's birthday.

6 Write about this picture.

7 Listen and say the chant.

What's in the shop?
A big black box.
What's in the box?
A big green bucket.
What's in the bucket?
A big blue shell.
What's in the shell?
Look! A little red fish.

Do or don't?

In the morning . . .

On the bus . . .

At school . . .

After school . . .

At the swimming pool . . .

Parents: see extra material on page 166

Reading and understanding

1 **Which picture? Match and say.**

A   B   C   D

E   F   G   H

1 On the bus … □   2 At the swimming pool … □

3 In the morning … □   4 Outdoors … □

5 In Grandma's garden … □   6 At night … □

7 At school … □   8 Indoors … □

2 **Read, circle and say.**

Remember: don't = do not

1   Get up!   Don't get up!

2   Stand up!   Don't stand up!

3   Run! Run!   Don't run!

4   Open the window.   Shut the window.

Get active   7

Comprehension focus   *consolidation of new language in Do or don't?*

Working with words

1 **Find the words.**

climblookjumpopenrunsit

2 **Write the words under the pictures.**

1

2

3

_____

4

5

6

Sentence building

A **verb** is a doing word.

jump   draw   run

1 **Read the sentences. Circle the verbs.**

1 Ben, open the window.

2 Tilly, climb the ladder.

3 Nina, look at the ball.

4 Sam, jump over the wall.

Grammar

Look at this!

Jump!

No! Don't jump!

1 **Match and say.**

1 Run! ☐

2 Please, sit down. ☐

3 Shut the door, please. ☐

4 Don't climb the tree! ☐

5 Don't write on the wall! ☐

2 **Write.**

| sit   Listen   fall   Look |

1 _____ to the bird!

2 Don't _____ !

3 Don't _____ down!

4 _____ at the butterfly!

Grammar focus _positive and negative commands_

Listening

1 **Listen and point.** 🎧

 Let's play Simon Says!

 Simon says, 'Stand up'.

 Simon says, 'Walk'.

 Simon says, 'Look at your friends'.

 Simon says, 'run'.

Stop!  Oh, no!

 Simon says 'Sit down'.

2 **Now play the game.**

3 **Listen, sing and do.** 🎧

Stand up! Sit down!	Stand up! Sit down!	Stand up! Sit down!
Stand up! Sit down!	Stand up! Sit down!	Stand up! Sit down!
Stand up!	Stand up!	Stand up!
Stamp your feet!	Stamp your feet!	Stamp your feet!
And sit down!	Clap your hands!	Clap your hands!
	And sit down!	Turn around!
		And sit down!

Phonics

1 **Listen and read.** 🎧

Children eat **ch**icken and **ch**ips for lun**ch**.

Children eat **ch**ocolate, mun**ch**, mun**ch**, mun**ch**!

2 **Say the sounds. Make the words.**

1

l   u   n   ch

_____

2

m   u   n   ch

_____

3 **Match and write the words. Circle the *ch* in each word.**

| chicken   children   chocolate   chips |

1    2    3    4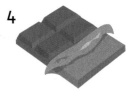

(ch)ildren   _____   _____   _____

4 **Tick ✓ the words you can read.**

children ☐   chips ☐   chicken ☐   chocolate ☐   lunch ☐   munch ☐

Class writing

1 **Match and write.**

Let's write rules.

Cross the road safely!

| Listen! Stop! Look all around! |
| Walk! Don't run! Look and listen! Wait! |

1 _Stop!_____

2 _____

3 _____

4 _____

5 _____

6 _____

Remember: Walk! ✔ Don't run! ✗

Where are the animals?

In the forest ...

An owl is sitting in a tree. It is brown and white.
It is very still. Where is it? Can you find it?
The butterflies are yellow and orange and red.
They are beautiful. Can you see them?
What are they doing?

In the jungle ...

The tiger is black and yellow. It can run very fast.
But now it is sleeping. Can you see it? Where is it?
A snake is sleeping, too.
It is black and green. Where is it?

Parents: see extra material on page 166

By the river ...

Be careful! There is a crocodile here.
It is swimming in the river. Can you see it?
What colour is it?
A big grey elephant is walking in the trees.
You can see its long trunk and big ears.
Can you find it?

In the snow ...

Some animals live in the cold ice and snow.
They are white. Can you find the white fox?
What is it doing? What is the polar bear doing?
What colour is it?

Reading and understanding

1 **Which sentences are about the picture? Read and ✓ tick.**

1 It is sitting in a tree. ☐

2 It is white. ☐

3 It can run very fast. ☐

4 There is ice and snow. ☐

5 It is swimming in the river. ☐

6 It is not running now. ☐

2 **Read and ✓ tick.**

1 It is cold.	ice ☐	snow ☐	the jungle ☐
2 They can be white.	foxes ☐	bears ☐	crocodiles ☐
3 They can be grey.	tigers ☐	hippos ☐	elephants ☐
4 They have got big ears.	hippos ☐	foxes ☐	elephants ☐

3 **What is it? Write the answer.**

1 It can be black, brown or white. It rhymes with chair. _____

2 They have got wings but they are not birds. _____

3 It is long and it hasn't got any legs. It rhymes with cake. _____

4 It is green and it can jump. It rhymes with dog. _____

Get active 8

Comprehension focus *consolidation of new language in* Where are the animals?

Working with words

1 **Read and number the animal names.**

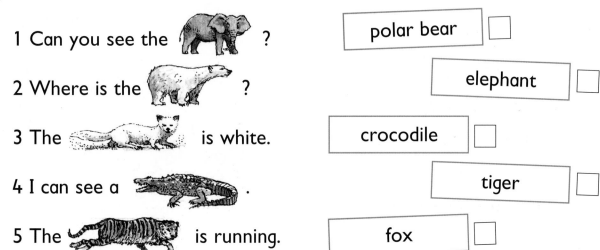

1 Can you see the [elephant] ?

2 Where is the [polar bear] ?

3 The [fox] is white.

4 I can see a [crocodile] .

5 The [tiger] is running.

polar bear ☐

elephant ☐

crocodile ☐

tiger ☐

fox ☐

Sentence building

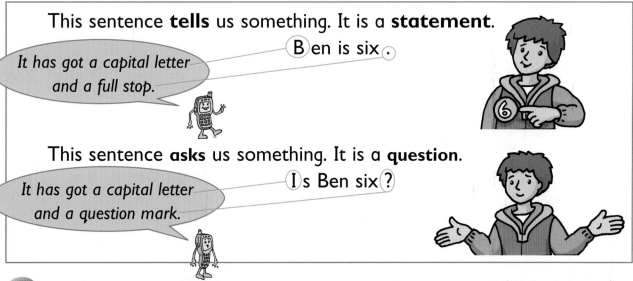

This sentence **tells** us something. It is a **statement**.

Ⓑen is six⊙

It has got a capital letter and a full stop.

This sentence **asks** us something. It is a **question**.

Ⓘs Ben six⑦

It has got a capital letter and a question mark.

1 **Read the sentences. Make these statements into questions.**

1 The elephant is red. _____

2 The boys are happy. _____

3 She is nine. _____

4 The dog is black. _____

Grammar

Look at this!

Look at the parrot. It is sitting in the tree.
Look at Ben. He is running.
Look at Nina. She is jumping.
Look at the monkeys. They are playing football.

1 **Circle Yes or No.**

1. The monkey is sleeping.   Yes   No

2. The girls are jumping.   Yes   No

3. The crocodile is swimming.   Yes   No

4. The children are sitting under a tree.   Yes   No

2 **Write.** | He is   She is   It is   They are |

1 _____ jumping.

2 _____ swimming.

3 _____ running.

4 _____ holding a monkey.

Grammar focus   *action verbs in the present continuous*

Listening

What are they doing?

1 **Listen and ✓ tick.**

1 He is swimming. ☐

He is running. ☐

2 They are sitting in the classroom. ☐

They are playing in the playground. ☐

3 She is holding a bird. ☐

She is holding a cat. ☐

4 It is climbing a tree. ☐

It is sleeping. ☐

2 **Listen, point and say.**

He is swimming.

3 **Listen and sing.**

Two little birds sitting on a wall.
Here is Peter. Here is Paul.
Fly away Peter. Fly away Paul.
Come back Peter. Come back Paul.

Phonics

1 **Listen and read.**

 On Monday,
I ring a be**ll**.

 On Tuesday,
I kick a ba**ll**.

On Wednesday,
I play with a do**ll**.

On Thursday,
I sit on a wa**ll**.

On Friday,
I climb a hi**ll**.

On Saturday,
I go to the ma**ll**.

2 **Match and write the words. Circle the _ll_ in each word.**

ball	bell	doll	hill	mall	wall

1

hi(ll)

2

3

4

5

6

3 **Write.**

1

Sam is in the _____ .

2

Sam has got a _____ and a _____ .

4 **Tick ✓ the words you can read.**

ball ☐   wall ☐   mall ☐   bell ☐   hill ☐   doll ☐

Phonics focus   *words with the ll sound and spelling*

Class writing

Let's write about doing things.

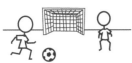  

playing   swimming   writing   running

sitting   jumping   singing   sleeping

1 Draw and write.

Look at the boy!   Look at the girl.   _____

He is playing.   She is running.   _____

_____   _____   _____

_____   _____   _____

_____   _____   _____

Remember! swi**mm**ing ru**nn**ing si**tt**ing

Writing focus describing action

Playtime

My friends and I are at school.
We are in the playground.
It is playtime. We are having fun!

Look at these boys.
They are marching
in a line.
Listen!

*Left, right,
left, right.*

*A pocket full
of posies.*

*Ring a ring
of roses.*

These girls are dancing
round in a ring.
They are holding hands
and they are singing.
Can you hear them?

*Atishoo!
Atishoo!*

*We all fall
down.*

Trit, trot!

Trit, trot!

What are these girls doing?
Are they riding horses?
Listen!

These boys are playing football. They are running up and down the playground.

These children are climbing on the climbing frame. Our teacher is watching them.

Be careful!

I like coffee. I like tea. I want Nadia in with me!

Here are my friends. Sara is skipping. What is she saying? Listen!

Brrrrrring!

Oh! It is the bell. Playtime is finished.

Reading and understanding

1 **Look at the pictures and write *Yes* or *No*.**

1

Are we dancing in a ring?

_____

2

Are we holding hands?

_____

3

Are we climbing?

_____

4

Are we marching in a line?

_____

2 **Read and number the pictures.**

1 She is skipping.

2 He is running.

3 They are playing football.

4 I am riding a horse.

5 We are singing.

6 She is sitting on a chair.

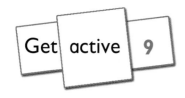

Working with words

1 **Ride, climb or play? Write the words.**

a horse

a tree

football

a bike

a game

a mountain

ride	climb	play

_____   _____   _____

_____   _____   _____

Sentence building

Verbs with **is** and **are** tell us what is happening now.

He **is** jumping.

They **are** running.

*Remember, a **verb** is a **doing** word.*

1 **Write *is* or *are*.**

1   The boy _____ swimming.

2   The boys _____ playing.

3   The cat _____ climbing.

4   The girls _____ clapping.

2 **Read the sentences.**

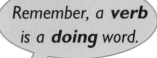

Grammar

 Look at this!

Is he riding a horse?

No, he isn't.

Is he riding an elephant?

Yes, he is.

Are they dancing?

No, they aren't.

Are they marching?

Yes, they are.

1 **Ask and answer.**

1

riding a bike?

2

playing a drum?

3

singing?

4

running?

2 **Read and ✓ tick.**

 ☐   ☐

 ☐   ☐

1 She is not running.   2 It is not sleeping.

 ☐   ☐

 ☐    ☐

3 They are not singing.   4 He is not riding a bike.

3 **Write.** | is not   are not |

1 Tilly _____ dancing.
2 Sam and Ben _____ playing drums.
3 The monkeys _____ singing.
4 Mobi _____ sleeping.

Grammar focus   *question and answer forms with the present continuous*

Listening

1 **Listen and point.**

I've got two little hands.

1   2   3   4   5   6

7   8   9   10   11   12

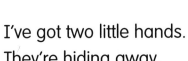

2 **Listen and do.**

3 **Listen and sing.**

I've got two little hands.
They're hiding away.
Now here comes one
and the other, to play!

Now they are clapping
And shaking and tapping.
They are rolling and pushing
And pulling and pointing.
To the right, to the left,
To the left, to the right.
And now they are going to bed.
Goodnight!

Phonics

1 **Listen and read.**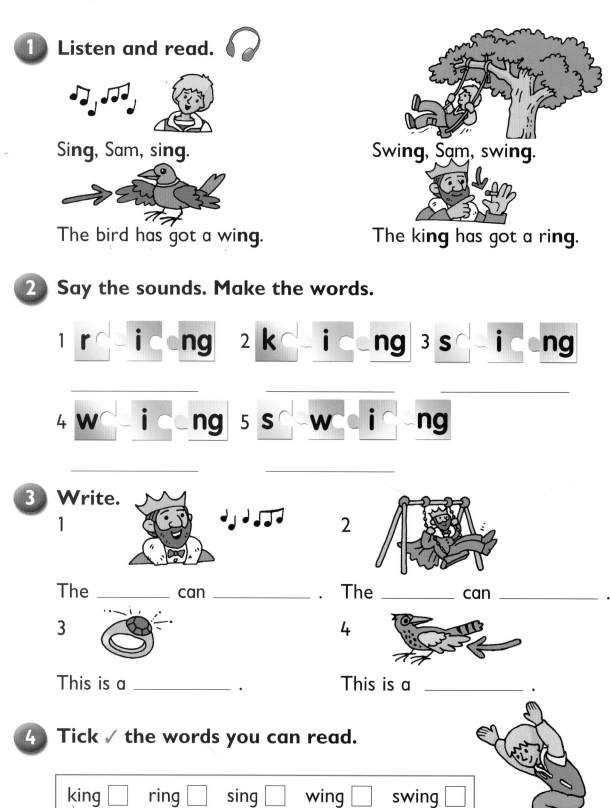

Si**ng**, Sam, si**ng**.

The bird has got a wi**ng**.

Swi**ng**, Sam, swi**ng**.

The ki**ng** has got a ri**ng**.

2 **Say the sounds. Make the words.**

1 r i ng   2 k i ng   3 s i ng

_____   _____

4 w i ng   5 s w i ng

_____   _____

3 **Write.**

1

The _____ can _____ .

2

The _____ can _____ .

3

This is a _____ .

4

This is a _____ .

4 **Tick ✓ the words you can read.**

king ☐   ring ☐   sing ☐   wing ☐   swing ☐

   Phonics focus   words with the **ng** sound and spelling

Class writing

Let's write about what people are doing.

1 **Point, ask and answer.**

This is Sam. Is he swimming?

No, he isn't.

 1 swimming?

 2 dancing?

 3 singing?

 4 riding?

 5 running?

 6 climbing?

2 **Now write.**

Is Sam swimming?   No, he is not.

_____   _____

_____   _____

Remember!   Is Sam swimming?   No, he is not.

Revision 3
You can do it!

1 Look at the picture.
What can you see?

2 Listen and read.

3 Read and say.
Point to Tilly:
Where is she?
What is she doing?
What is Mobi saying?

Point to Ben:
Where is he?
What is he doing?
What is Ben saying?
What is Mobi saying?

Point to Sam:
Where is he?
What is he doing?
What is Mobi saying?

Who is on the elephant?
What is she doing?
What is Mobi saying?

Who is under a tree?
What is she doing?
Who has got balloons?
What colour are they?

Tilly is on the swing.
She is swinging very high.

Be careful!

Ben is on the bridge.
He is running very fast.

Stop!
Don't run!

Look at me!

Don't fall!

Sam is on the climbing frame.

Miss Plum is sitting under a tree. She is holding four balloons. Who are they for?

Come here, children!

Where's my balloon?

Sit down, Nina.

Nina is riding on an elephant. She is standing up.

4   Listen, point and say who Mobi is talking to.

5   Finish the story. Say who the balloons are for.

6   Act out the story.

7   Listen and say the chant.

Chicken and chips,
Chicken and chips.
We all love chicken and chips.
Ring the bells!
Bang the drums!
It's chicken and chips
for lunch!
HOORAY!

Suki's day

It's Saturday.
It's seven o'clock.
Good morning, Suki!
Suki is still sleepy.

It's ten o'clock.
Suki is playing with her friends.
She's very happy!

It's half past twelve.
Say goodbye to your friends!
Suki is a little bit sad.

Time for lunch!

Parents: *see extra material on page 166*

It's three o'clock.
Suki is thirsty.
Milk and a cake. Yummy!

It's half past five.
Suki is hungry.
Hooray! Pizza for dinner!

It's half past seven.
Suki is very, very, very tired.
Goodnight, Suki!

I wake in the morning early
And always, the very first thing,
I poke out my head
And I sit up in bed
And I sing and I sing and I sing.

Rose Fyleman

Reading and understanding

1 **Look and read. Then circle the words.**

1  Suki is thirsty.
hungry.

2  She is tired.
sad.

3 She is hungry.
happy.

4 She is tired.
thirsty.

5 She is sad.
happy.

2 **Read and match.**

a

b

c

d

e

f

1 It's three o'clock. ☐

2 It's half past nine. ☐

3 It's seven o'clock. ☐

4 It's twelve o'clock. ☐

5 It's half past eleven. ☐

6 It's ten o'clock. ☐

3 **Read and complete the poem.**

| thing | early | bed | sing | head |

I wake in the morning _____
And always, the very first _____,
I poke out my_____
And I sit up in _____
And I sing and I sing and I _____.

Can you find the
rhyming words?

Get active 10

Comprehension focus *consolidation of new language in Suki's day*

Working with words

1 **Find and write the words.**

1
2
3

5

4

4
5

2 **Write sentences.**

1
2
3

He _____   _____   _____

Sentence building

The days of the week are **proper nouns**.

Monday   **T**uesday   **W**ednesday

> Proper nouns begin with a capital letter.

1 **Begin each proper noun with the correct capital letter.**

| ☐aturday | ☐unday | ☐onday | ☐uesday |

| ☐ednesday | ☐hursday | ☐riday |

Grammar

one
three
five
seven
nine
eleven

two
four
six
eight
ten
twelve

What's the time?

It's nine o'clock.

What's the time?

It's half past three.

1 Point, ask and answer.

1   2   3

Remember!
What's = What is
It's = It is

4   5   6

2 Write.

1 It is _____ o'clock.

2 It is _____ o'clock.

3 It is _____ o'clock.

4 It is half past _____.

5 It is half past _____.

6 It is half past _____.

Listening

Listen to Harry's week.

1 **Listen and match.**

Monday	
Tuesday	
Wednesday	
Thursday	
Friday	
Saturday	
Sunday	

a

b

c

d

e

f

g

2 **Listen again and talk about the boy.**

It's Monday.
He's in a car with his dad.

swimming
on the beach
playing football
at the playground
riding an elephant

3 **Listen and say.**

The big town clock goes:
TICK TOCK, TICK TOCK.
The kitchen clock goes:
Tick tock, tick tock, tick tock, tick tock.
Grandpa's little pocket watch goes:
Ticka tocka, ticka tocka, ticka tocka, ticka tocka tick.

Phonics

1 **Listen and read.** 🎧

The clo**ck** on the ro**ck** says ti**ck** to**ck**.

The clo**ck** in the so**ck** says ti**ck** to**ck**.

The du**ck** in the sa**ck** says qua**ck** qua**ck**.

The du**ck** on the ro**ck** says qua**ck** qua**ck**.

2 **Say the sounds. Make the words.**

| s | o | ck | r | o | ck | c | l | o | ck |

1 _____   2 _____   3 _____

| t | i | ck | d | u | ck | qu | a | ck |

4 _____   5 _____   6 _____

3 **Write.**

1   2   3

A _____ says   The _____ is   The _____ is
tick _____.   on the _____.   in the _____.

4 **Tick ✓ the words you can read.**

rock ☐   sock ☐   clock ☐   sack ☐   quack ☐
duck ☐   tick ☐   tock ☐

Class writing

Let's write about days of the week.

Day	**Time**	**Place**
Monday		 at home
Tuesday		at school
Wednesday	two o'clock	on the beach
Thursday		at the playground
Friday		in a car
Saturday	half past two	in a plane
Sunday		

1 **Choose a day, a time and a place. Draw and write.**

1   This is Sam.

It is <u>Friday</u>.
It is <u>five o'clock</u>.
He is <u>at the playground</u>.

2   This is Tilly.

It is _____.
It is _____.
She is _____.

3 [ ]   This is me.

_____.
_____.
_____.

Here comes the train!

clickety clack

The train

Here comes the train!
It is going very fast.
Listen! The train is making a noise.
Can you hear it?

On the train

People are sitting on the train.
What are they doing?
Some people are reading and some are talking.
Some people are listening to music,
and some are looking out of the window.
Some people are also eating and drinking.
You can buy food on a train.

Parents: *see extra material on page 167*

Here comes a man.
He is checking
the tickets.

In the town

Now the train is
in the town.
Listen!

Here is the station. The train is stopping.
The doors are opening. The people are getting off.
They are walking very fast! Everyone is in a hurry!

Reading and understanding

1 **Read and find. Then number the pictures.**

1 The train is making a noise.

2 Some people are reading.

3 Some people are looking out
of the window.

4 A woman is drinking water.

5 You can buy food on a train.

Clickety clack

2 **Read the questions. Match the questions and answers.**

 1   What is it doing? ☐   a He is checking the tickets.

 2   What are they doing? ☐   b They are talking.

 3   What is she doing? ☐   c It is going very fast.

4   What is he doing? ☐   d She is eating crisps.

Remember!   ge**tt**ing off   sto**pp**ing   si**tt**ing

Get active   11

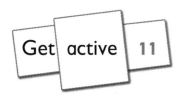

Working with words

1 **Write the words.**

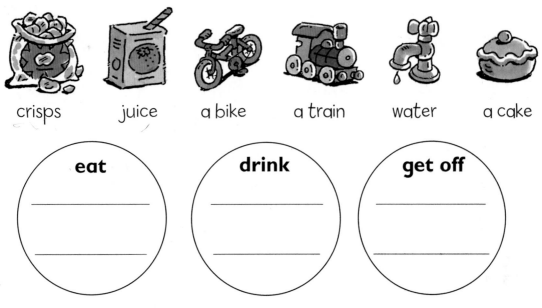

crisps   juice   a bike   a train   water   a cake

eat
_____
_____

drink
_____
_____

get off
_____
_____

Sentence building

You can use a **pronoun** instead of a noun.

Remember, a noun is a naming word.

The **girl** is running.   **She** is running.

noun   pronoun

1 **Write a pronoun from the box instead of the underlined noun.**

He	She	They	It

1 <u>The dog</u> is running.   _____ is running.
2 <u>The boys</u> are reading.   _____ are reading.
3 <u>Ben</u> is riding his bike.   _____ is riding his bike.
4 <u>Nina</u> is playing football.   _____ is playing football.

Grammar

What is he doing?

He's swimming.

What is she doing?

She's riding.

What are they doing?

They're playing football.

What are you doing, Mobi?

Shhh! I'm sleeping.

Remember!
I'm = I am
he's = he is
she's = she is
they're = they are

1 Write and ask questions. Answer with words from the box.

1

<u>What is</u> he <u>doing</u> ?

2

_____ she _____ ?

3

_____ they _____ ?

4

_____ she _____ ?

5

_____ they _____ ?

6

_____ he _____ ?

running

fishing

eating

reading

climbing

singing

Listening

People are getting off the train.

1 **Look and listen. Listen again and point.** 🎧

2 **Now point and say.**

3 **Listen and say.** 🎧

Can you see the engines
Standing in a row
Waiting at the station
Till they hear the whistle blow?

'Whee!' goes the whistle,
And off they puff -
Toot-toot, clank-clank,
Chuff-chuff-chuff!

Richard Dungworth

Phonics

1 **Listen and read.**

The **br**ick is **br**own.   The **cr**ab is **br**own.   The **dr**ink is **br**own, too.

The **gr**ass is **gr**een.   The **tr**uck is **gr**een.   The **dr**ess for the queen is blue!

2 **Say the sounds. Make the words.**

| br | cr | tr | cr | gr | dr | tr | br |

1 <u>br</u> ick   2 ___ ab   3 ___ ass   4 ___ uck

3 **Write.**

1 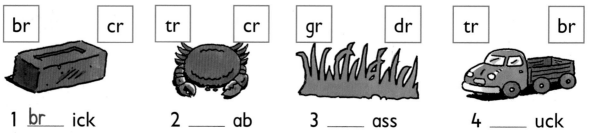   2

The _____ is _____.   The _____ is _____.

4 **Tick ✓ the words you can read.**

brick ☐   brown ☐   crab ☐   dress ☐   drink ☐

grass ☐   green ☐   truck ☐

Phonics focus   *words beginning with the* **br cr dr gr** *or* **tr** *sound*

Class writing

Let's write about activities!

1 **Write a word for a friend to act out.**

> swimming   riding a bike   dancing   eating   drinking
> playing football   walking   running   sitting

What's she doing?

She's running.

2 **Point, ask and answer.**

1    2    3

4    5    6

3 **Choose three pictures. Write questions.**
Your friend writes answers.

☐ 5 What is it doing?   ☐ _____

      It is eating.   _____

☐ _____   ☐ _____

_____   _____

> Remember!   What **is** he/she/it doing?   What **are** they doing?

We all love the mall

This is a great clothes shop. Girls' clothes are upstairs. Boys' clothes are downstairs.

This toy shop is quite small. It's got lots of toy cars and trains and computer games. It's got a slide.

There is a computer shop. This shop has got great computers. You can buy a green computer or a purple computer or, of course, grey or black.

'Happy Books' is a children's bookshop. There's a very big book in the window.

There is a children's shoe shop. Look at all the shoes. There are trainers and boots and sandals.

Clothes

Girls' clothes

Clothes

Boys' clothes

Toys

Computers

Bikes

Happy Books

Children's Sho

There are lovely smells in the cake shop. There are buns and cakes and biscuits. Yum!

There are lots of restaurants at the mall. This restaurant is 'Gino's Place'. It's got delicious pizzas.

There are two bike shops. You can buy children's bikes at this shop. There are big bikes, small bikes and BMXs.

This is a sweet shop. The chocolates are yummy. You can buy lovely presents here for mum or dad. It's also got ice creams!

There is one supermarket in the mall. It's enormous. You can buy food, clothes, toys, books and flowers.

Reading and understanding

1 **Read and circle answer A or B.**

		A	B
1	There are lots of these in the mall.	restaurants	supermarkets
2	You can buy computer games here.	bookshop	toy shop
3	There are two of these shops.	bike shops	shoe shops
4	Girls can shop upstairs in this shop.	clothes shop	bookshop
5	There are lots of chocolates in this shop.	sweet shop	toy shop
6	You can buy flowers here.	supermarket	bookshop
7	You can buy delicious pizzas here.	sweet shop	Gino's place

2 **Read, look and circle true (T) or false (F).**

1 There is a clown.   T   F

2 There are four ice creams.   T   F

3 There are five people.   T   F

4 There are ten balloons.   T   F

5 There is a toy shop.   T   F

6 There is a supermarket.   T   F

3 **Play a game: What can you buy at the mall?**

At the mall I can buy toys.

At the mall I can buy toys and games.

At the mall I can buy toys, games and ...

Get active 12

Working with words

1 **Look and write the words.**

1    2    3

| cake shop |
| bike shop |
| shoe shop |
| sweet shop |
| clothes shop |
| toy shop |

4    5    6

Sentence building

A **preposition** can tell us **where something is**.

The ball is **on** the box.   It is **in** the box.   It is **under** the box.

The ball is **behind** the box.   It is **next to** the box.

1 **Read the sentences. Underline the prepositions.**

1 The doll is on the chair.   2 The cat is under the bed.

3 The dog is in the box.   4 The toys are behind the bed.

5 The teddy is next to the table.

Grammar

Look at this!

There are lots of toys in the toyshop.

There's a ball.

There's a train.

There are dolls.

There are computer games.

There's = There is

1 **What can you see in the toy shop? Point and say.**

There's a ball.

There are dolls.

2 **Read and circle.**

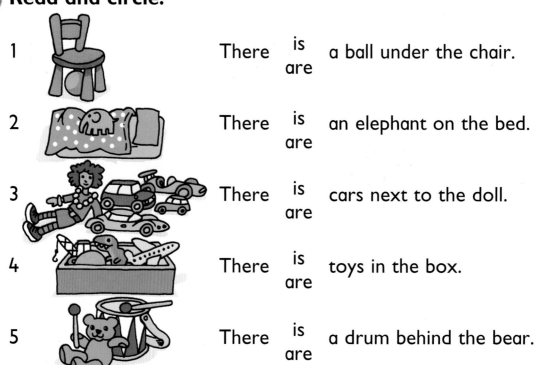

1   There   is / are   a ball under the chair.

2   There   is / are   an elephant on the bed.

3   There   is / are   cars next to the doll.

4   There   is / are   toys in the box.

5   There   is / are   a drum behind the bear.

Listening

Where are they?

1 **Listen, point and answer the question.**

The shoe shop

The toy shop

The computer shop

The bike shop

The cafe

2 **Listen and sing.**

Tall shop in the town,
Lifts moving up and down,
Doors swinging round about,
People moving in and out.

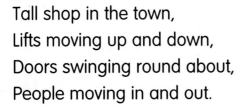

Phonics

1 **Listen and read.**

The **cl**own has got a **bl**ue **fl**ag,
a red **fl**ower and one **bl**ack shoe.

The **cl**own has got a yellow **pl**ate and a
yellow **gl**ass but the **pl**ane is **bl**ue.

2 **Say the sounds. Make the words.**

| bl | | gl | cl | | pl | gl | | fl | pl | | cl |

1 ___ ass   2 ___ own   3 ___ ower   4 ___ ane

3 **Write and colour.**

1

2

3

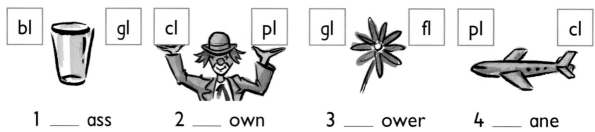

The _____ is blue.   The _____ is black.   The _____ is blue.

4 **Tick ✓ the words you can read.**

| black ☐ | blue ☐ | clown ☐ | flag ☐ |
| flower ☐ | glass ☐ | plane ☐ | plate ☐ |

Class writing

Let's write about a park.

1 **Draw and colour these things in the big picture.**

an owl   a girl   a boy   birds   bees   kites

2 **Now write about the park.**

This is a lovely park. There is a green frog on the slide.
There are white ducks on the pond.

_____

_____

_____

_____

_____

_____

Writing focus   description using prepositions of place

111

Revision 4

You can do it!

1 **Look at the pictures.** Is there a sports club near you? Do you like it? What can you do there, and when?

2 **Listen and read.**

3 **Read and say.**
Look at the football game.
What day and time is it?
Who is playing? How many points has each team got?

Look at Nina and Tilly. What are they doing? What day and time is it?

Who is riding his bike? Where is he? What day and time is it?

Who is having a birthday party? How old is she? How many children are there? What day and time is it?

What is happening this week:

Saturday   Sunday   Monday   Tuesday

football   swimming   cycling   basketball

It is Saturday. It is 3 o'clock. There is a football match. Sam and Ben are in the red team. Who is winning?

It is Wednesday. It is 1 o'clock. Nina and Tilly are playing tennis. Where is the ball?

It is Monday. It is 4 o'clock. Ben is riding his bike. Is he going fast?

Wednesday   Thursday   Friday

tennis   trampoline   birthday party

Look at Miss Plum.
What is she doing?
What day and time is it?
Can you swim?
Are you a good swimmer?

What is Mobi doing on Thursday? What time is it? Can you jump? Do you like it?

4 **Listen and say the day and the time.**

5 **Choose a picture and act it out. Your friends guess.**

6 **Listen and say the chant.**

Ha ha!
Look at the clowns.
Brrm! Brrm!
They're in a truck.
Quack! Quack!
They've got a duck.
Tick tock!
They've got a clock.
Ha ha!
Look at the clowns!

It is Friday. It is 6 o'clock. There are lots of children at a party. It is Lucy's birthday. How old is she?

It is Sunday. It is half past 9. Miss Plum is swimming. Is she a good swimmer?

It is Thursday. It is half past seven. Look at Mobi! He is jumping. Is he having fun?

Dani can count!

This is Sami. These are his father's sheep.
Sami is looking after them on the hillside.
Today, his younger brother, Dani is here, too.
Sami is pointing to the sheep in front of them.
'Look at these sheep,' he says.
'How many are there?' asks Dani.
'I don't know,' says Sami.

I can count all these sheep, Sami!

Can you?

Yes! One, two, three, four, five, six, seven … Hmmmm …

Eight.

Oh, yes. Eight, nine, ten, eleven, twelve, thirteen …

Parents: see extra material on page 167

Reading and understanding

1 **Find the mistakes. Write the sentences.**

1 Dani is Sami's big brother.
2 Sami is looking after his brother's sheep.
3 They are on a mountain.
4 Sami has got a cat.
5 'How many sheep are there?' asks Sami.
6 Dani can count to forty.

2 **Read and match.**

1 fifty ☐
2 twenty ☐
3 ten ☐
4 eighty ☐
5 thirty ☐
6 one hundred ☐

We can also say **a** hundred.

3 **Listen and circle.**

| 1 | **13 30** | 2 | **16 60** | 3 | **18 80** |
| 4 | **14 40** | 5 | **17 70** | 6 | **19 90** |

Get active 13

Comprehension focus *consolidation of new language in Dani can count!*

Working with words

1 **Read the numbers down, then across.**

one	eleven	ten
two	twelve	twenty
three	thirteen	thirty
four	fourteen	forty
five	fifteen	fifty
six	sixteen	sixty
seven	seventeen	seventy
eight	eighteen	eighty
nine	nineteen	ninety

Sentence building

This is the verb **to have**:

I have / I've   we have / we've
you have / you've   you have / you've
he has / he's   they have / they've
she has / she's
it has / it's

I've got an apple.

1 **Complete the sentences with *have* or *has*.**

1 He _____ got a brother.   2 She _____ got a doll.
3 They _____ got ice creams.   4 Ben _____ got a dog.
5 The boys _____ got computer games.

2 **Read the sentences.**

Grammar

Look at this!

How many castles are there?

1 **Count and write the numbers.**

1 [2]

2 [ ]

3 [ ]

4  [ ]

5 [ ]

6 [ ]

2 **Ask and answer.**

castles   stars   trees   birds   boys   girls

How many castles are there?

There are two castles.

3 **Look again at the picture. Write Tilly's questions.**

1 How many _____? _Four._
2 _____? _Six._
3 _____? _Five._
4 _____? _Seven_

Listening

How many are there?

1 **Listen and circle the number.** 🎧

1

17   18
19   20

2

11   12
13   14

3

2   5
7   10

4

80   90
99   100

5

24   25
26   27

Phonics

1 Listen and read. 🎧

Do you like **th**in or **th**ick pizza best?

Look! I've got **th**ree eggs in my nest.

I've got **th**irteen ducks in my ba**th**.

I've got **th**irty-**th**ree ants on my pa**th**!

2 Match and write the word. Circle the *th* in each word.

thick	thin	bath	path	path	bath	thin	thick

1 _____ 2 _____ 3 _____ 4 _____

3 Match and write the words. Circle the *th* in each word.

three
thirteen
thirty

3   **13**   **30**

_____   _____   _____

4 Tick ✓ the words you can read.

three ☐ thirteen ☐ thirty ☐ thick ☐ thin ☐

bath ☐ path ☐

Class writing

Let's write about our classroom.

1 **How many are there in your classroom? Count and write.**

windows ☐   doors ☐   desks ☐   chairs ☐   boards ☐

pictures ☐   teachers ☐   children ☐   boys ☐   girls ☐

2 **Ask and answer.**

How many windows are there?

There are ... windows.

Remember!
There **is a** board.
There **are** windows.

3 **Write about your classroom.**

In my classroom there is _____

and there are _____

_____

_____

_____

Splish, splash, splosh

boom-er-room-er-room!

'It's Monday. We're going shopping,' says Mum.
'Oh! It's windy,' says Sue.
'Woooooooooooooooooooo,' says Sally.

'Stop, Susan,' says Mum. 'Don't do that!'
Susan is splashing in the puddles.
'Splish, splash, splosh,' says Sally.

'Look at that black cloud,' says Mum.
'I can hear thunder,' says Sue.
'Boom-er-room-er-room,' says Sally.

'Let's hurry,' says Mum.
'Oh, no! It's raining,' says Sue.
'Pit, pat, pit, pat,' says Sally.

'Uh oh, there's lightning,' says Mum.
'Kerash,' says Sally.
'I'm scared,' says Sue.

'Here's the supermarket,' says Mum.
'Let's go inside,' says Sue.
'Awwwwww,' says Sally. 'I like the weather noises!'

Reading and understanding

1 **Read and circle true (T) or false (F).**

1 Mum, Sally and Sue are going shopping.   T   F
2 Mum says, 'Don't do that!'   T   F
3 It is snowing.   T   F
4 Sally is scared.   T   F
5 It is cloudy.   T   F
6 Sue likes weather noises.   T   F

Remember!
It is rain**ing**. It is snow**ing**.

2 **Read and match.**

a    b    c

d    e    f

1 It is windy.   ☐

2 Sue is splashing in the puddles.   ☐

3 It is raining.   ☐

4 Look at that black cloud.   ☐

5 I can hear thunder.   ☐

6 There's lightning.   ☐

Get active 14

Comprehension focus   *consolidation of new language in* Splish, splash, splosh!

14

Working with words

1 **Look at the pictures and write.**

foggy	cloudy	sunny
windy	raining	snowing

1

It is _____.

2

It is _____.

3

It is _____.

4

It is _____.

5

It is _____.

6

It is _____.

2 **Find and circle the words.**

rainglsnowdpcloudnbfogrqwindapthundervosunxilightningt

Sentence building

An **adjective** is a **describing** word.
It tells us more about a **noun**.

a **red** box   a **cloudy** day   a **long** snake   a **small** mouse

1 **Read the sentences. Circle the adjectives.**

1 This is a new bed.   2 This is a big desk.

3 This is a pink doll.   4 It is a windy day.

2 **Underline the nouns.**

Language focus *weather words; adjectives*

Grammar

It is raining.   It is snowing.   It is cold.   It is hot.

It is sunny.   It is cloudy.   It is windy.   It is foggy.

1 **Ask and answer.**

What's the weather like today?

Is it cold?

Is it snowing?

Yes, it is.

No, it isn't.

cloudy?   hot?   raining?   sunny?   foggy?   windy?

2 **Read and write.**

1 Wear your 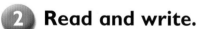 sunglasses. It is _____ today.

2 Take an umbrella. _____

3 Hold on to your hat. _____

4 Let's have an ice cream. _____

Listening

What's the weather like?

1 **Listen and draw the weather.**

1  2  3

4  5  6

2 **Now talk about the pictures.**

Tilly and Nina are in the treehouse. What's the weather like?

It's snowing.

3 **Listen and sing.**

Oh, Mr Sun, Sun, Mr Golden Sun,
Won't you please shine down on me?
Oh, Mr Sun, Sun, Mr Golden Sun,
You are hiding behind a tree.
These little children are asking you,
Please come out so we can play with you.
Oh, Mr Sun, Sun, Mr Golden Sun,
Won't you please shine down on me?

Phonics

1 **Listen and read.** 🎧

Stop.   **Sm**ell.   **Sw**im.   **Sp**ell.

Pick up a **sp**ider.   Pick up a **sn**ake.   Pick up a **sw**eet
                                                  from the plate.

2 **Say the sounds. Make the words.**

st ▸ op	sw ▸ im	sp ▸ ell	sm ▸ ell
1 _____	2 _____	3 _____	4 _____

sn ▸ ake	sw ▸ eet	sp ▸ ider
5 _____	6 _____	7 _____

3 **Write.**

1   2   3

This is my _____.   This is my _____.   This is my _____.

4 **Tick ✓ the words you can read.**

stop ☐   swim ☐   sweet ☐   spell ☐

spider ☐   smell ☐   snake ☐

Class writing

Let's write about the weather.

1 **Point, ask and answer.**

It's Monday.
What's the weather like?

It's snowing and it's cold.

Monday   Tuesday   Wednesday

Thursday   Friday   Saturday

2 **Look at the pictures and write in the weather diary.**

Monday: Today it is snowing and cold.	Tuesday: _____ _____
Wednesday: _____ _____	Thursday: _____ _____
Friday: _____ _____	Saturday: _____ _____

Animal puzzles

I've got
long arms and
a long tail.
What am I?

We're soft and white.
We've got long ears
and fluffy tails.
What are we?

Look at my
big mouth.
I can swim.
I've got
little ears.
What am I?

We've got big
ears and long noses.
We're very,
very big.
What are we?

I'm a giraffe!

We're rabbits!

I'm a monkey!

Parents: see extra material on page 167

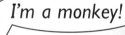

I've got very long legs and a very long neck. I like to eat leaves for my dinner. What am I?

We're owls!

We've got short legs. Our feet are orange and we love to swim. What are we?

We live in trees and we fly at night. We've got big eyes. What are we?

We're ducks!

We're elephants!

I'm a hippo!

What have they got?

131

Reading and understanding

1 **Answer the questions.**

1 They are soft and they have got fluffy tails. What are they?

2 It is very big and it has got big ears. What is it?

3 They have got very long arms. What are they?

4 It has got a long neck and it likes to eat leaves. What is it?

5 They have got orange feet and they love to swim. What are they?

6 It lives in a tree and it flies at night. What is it?

7 It has got a big mouth and little ears. What is it?

2 **Read and number the pictures.**

1 I'm a monkey!

2 I'm a giraffe!

3 We're rabbits!

4 I'm a hippo!

5 We're elephants!

6 We're owls!

7 We're ducks!

Get active 15

Comprehension focus *consolidation of new language in Animal puzzles*

Working with words

1 **Write about your body.**

| eye foot ear nose head body |
| hand arm leg knee shoulder |

| I've got one … | I've got two … |

2 **Write an animal.**

1 It has got a tail. _____
2 It has got long ears. _____
3 It has got a big mouth. _____
4 It has got big eyes. _____

Sentence building

This is the verb **to be**:

I am / I'm   we are / we're
you are / you're   you are / you're
he is / he's   they are / they're
she is / she's
it is / it's

I am Mobi!

1 **Complete the sentences with *am* or *is* or *are*.**

1 I _____ a monkey.
2 He _____ a giraffe.
3 She _____ a hippo.
4 They _____ rabbits.
5 We _____ ducks.

2 **Read the sentences.**

Grammar

Look at this!

Look at the elephants! They've got long trunks.

We haven't got trunks. We've got little noses.

Remember!
they've = they have
we've = we have
haven't = have not

1 **What have we got? What have elephants got? Tick ✓ the boxes.**

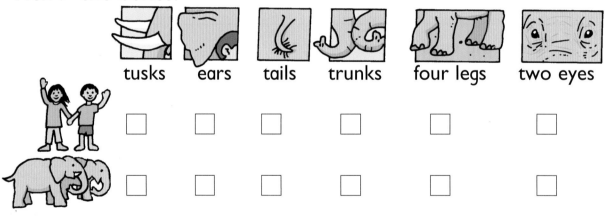

tusks	ears	tails	trunks	four legs	two eyes
☐	☐	☐	☐	☐	☐
☐	☐	☐	☐	☐	☐

2 **Ask and answer about elephants.**

 Have they got tusks?

 Yes, they have.

3 **Ask and answer about you and your friends.**

 Have we got trunks?

 No, we haven't.

Listening

What are the animals?

1 **Listen, point and say.**

1

zebras

2

giraffes

3

monkeys

4

lions

5

elephants

6

crocodiles

2 **Listen and say.**

Take . . .
A head, some shoulders, knees and toes,
A mouth and eyes that see,
A pair of legs, two feet, one nose,
And what you've got is
ME!

Theresa Heine

Phonics

1 Listen and read.

There is a b**nd** on the s**and**.

There is a sweet in my h**and**.

There is an a**nt** in my si**nk**.

My elepha**nt** is pi**nk**!

2 Say the sounds. Make the words.

ha → nd	ba → nd	sa → nd	a → nt
1 _____	2 _____	3 _____	4 _____

elepha → nt	si → nk	pi → nk
5 _____	6 _____	7 _____

3 Write.

1   2 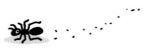   3

This is my _____.   This is an _____.   This is a _____.

4 Tick ✓ the words you can read.

hand ☐   sand ☐   band ☐   pink ☐

sink ☐   ant ☐   elephant ☐

Phonics focus *words ending with the* **nd nk** *or* **nt** *sound*

Class writing

 Let's write about animals.

 15

1 **Complete and colour the pictures. Then write about them.**

1

2

It is an elephant. It is grey.
It has got ears and a trunk.

_____
_____
_____

3

4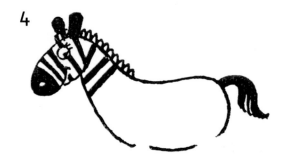

_____   _____
_____   _____
_____   _____

Remember!   It **has** got …   They **have** got …

Revision 5

You can do it!

1 **Look at the pictures.** What and who can you see? Where are they?

2 **Listen and read.** 🎧

3 **Read and say.**

Look at picture 1: Where are Ben and Nina? What's the weather like? What has Nina got?

Look at picture 2: Who can you see? Where are they? What's the weather like?

Look at picture 3: Where are Ben and Sam? Is it raining? What are the boys doing?

Look at picture 4: What's the weather like? Who can you see? Where are they?

Look at picture 5: What's the weather like? Can Ben and Sam see all the island? What can they see?

In this photo it is hot and sunny. Ben and Nina are on the beach. They are very happy. Nina has got an ice cream.

Sam and Ben are on the mountain. It is snowing and it is very cold. The boys are playing in the snow. Ben has got a big snowball.

Ben and Sam are at the top of the tall tree. It is very foggy. They can't see the jungle. They can see the top of the mountain. They can see Miss Plum, too.

Miss Plum and the children are on the sea. They are in two little boats. It is very windy. Tilly is cold.

It is cloudy today. The sky is grey. Nina and Tilly are on the big ship. Mr Fun, the clown, has got lots of balloons. How many balloons are there?

The children are riding on an elephant. It is raining and it is very windy. They are under a big umbrella. Mobi has got a little umbrella.

Look at picture 6: Is it windy? Is it snowing? What are the children doing? What is Nina holding?

4 **Find and say the numbers.**

5 **Listen, point and say which picture.** 🎧

6 **Choose a photo and act it out. Your friends guess.**

7 **Listen and say the chant.** 🎧

A spider in the bath. Help! A snake on the path. Help! A big pink elephant swimming in the sea – with me! HELP!

Let's have a picnic!

Summertime, summertime,
We all love summertime.
When the sun is hot and the sky is blue,
This is what we like to do.
We find a cool place under a tree
And we have a picnic,
Mum and Dad
    and Grandma and Grandpa
       and Uncle Charlie and Auntie Betty
        and Milly and Billy
         and Polly and Molly
          – and me!

Here's our basket!
What have we got?
Look at this!
There's such a lot!

Crunch on an apple,
Munch on a grape.
Here are the biscuits.
Yum! Have a cake.

Here are the sandwiches.
Have one of these.
Do you like orange juice?
Oh, yes, please!

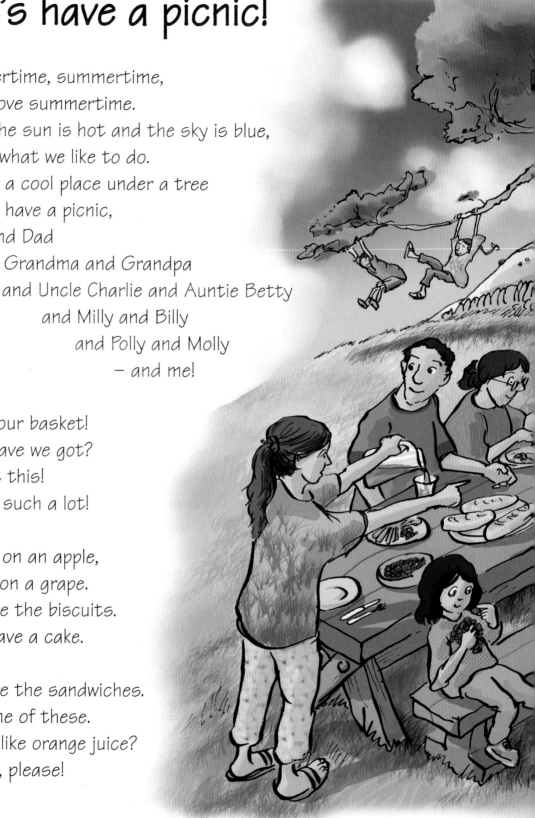

 Parents: see extra material on page 167

Summertime, summertime,
We all love summertime.
When the sun is hot and the sky is blue,
This is what we like to do.
We find a cool place under a tree
And we have a picnic,
Mum and Dad
    and Grandma and Grandpa
        and Uncle Charlie and Auntie Betty
            and Milly and Billy
                and Polly and Molly
                    – and me!

Reading and understanding

1 **Complete the sentences.**

basket	apple	sandwiches	sky	picnic
cakes	sun	orange juice	tree	grape

1 The _____ is hot and the _____ is blue.

2 It's cool under this _____ .

3 It's nice to have a _____ in the summertime.

4 Here is our _____ . What's inside?

5 Have one of these little pink _____ .

6 Crunch on an _____ . Munch on a _____ .

7 Here are the _____ . Have one of these.

8 The _____ is nice and cold.

2 **Read and circle ☺ or ☹ .**

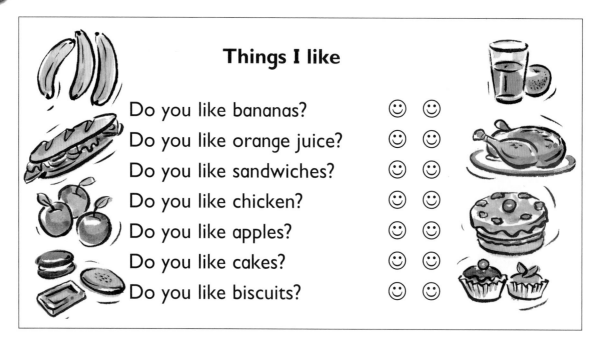

Things I like

Do you like bananas? ☺ ☺

Do you like orange juice? ☺ ☺

Do you like sandwiches? ☺ ☺

Do you like chicken? ☺ ☺

Do you like apples? ☺ ☺

Do you like cakes? ☺ ☺

Do you like biscuits? ☺ ☺

Get active 16

Comprehension focus *consolidation of new language in* Let's have a picnic!

Working with words

1 **Find the words.**

bananachickengrapesandwichjuicecakeorangebiscuitapple

How many things can you eat? ☐
How many things can you drink? ☐

Sentence building

> Remember, a noun is a naming word.

A **singular** noun is **one** thing.

book

A **plural** noun is **more than one** thing.

books

1 **Complete the table.**

singular noun	plural noun
one cup	two _____
one _____	three dogs
one orange	five _____
one _____	two baskets
one apple	four _____

Grammar

Look at this!

I like grapes.

Look at Sam.
He likes sandwiches.

Look at Tilly.
She likes cakes.

1 **Point and say.**

He likes
ice cream.

She likes
orange juice.

apples   ice cream   biscuits   bananas   chicken   orange juice.

2 **Complete the sentences.**

1 _____ orange juice.

2 _____ sandwiches.

3 _____ ice cream.

3 **Write about what food you like.**

I like _____

_____

Listening

Mobi likes everything!

1 **Listen and point. Then listen and tick ✓.** 🎧

apples						
grapes						
bananas						
chicken						
sandwiches						
orange juice						
cake						
biscuits						

2 **Point and say.**

3 **Listen and sing.** 🎧

I like the flowers, I love the daffodils.
I like the mountains, I love the grassy hills.
I like the fireside when all the lights are low.
Boom-tiara, boom-tiara, boom-tiara, boom!

Phonics

1 **Listen and read.** 🎧

I make a cake.

My cake is on a plate.

My plate is on the gate.

I like my bike.

I ride my bike.

I hide my bike.

2 **Say the sounds. Make the words. Match the rhymes.**

c ▸	ake	_cake_	pl ▸	ate	_____
g ▸	ate	_____	m ▸	ake	_make_
b ▸	ike	_____	h ▸	ide	_____
r ▸	ide	_____	l ▸	ike	_____

3 **Tick ✓ the words you can read.**

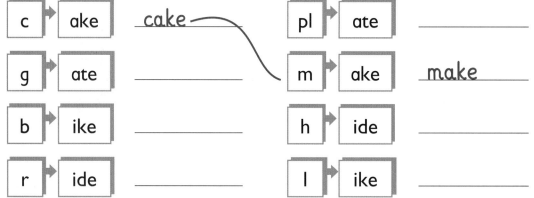

cake ☐ make ☐ gate ☐ plate ☐

ride ☐ hide ☐ like ☐ bike ☐

Phonics focus   *words with the spelling pattern a_e or i_e*

Class writing

Let's write about food we like!

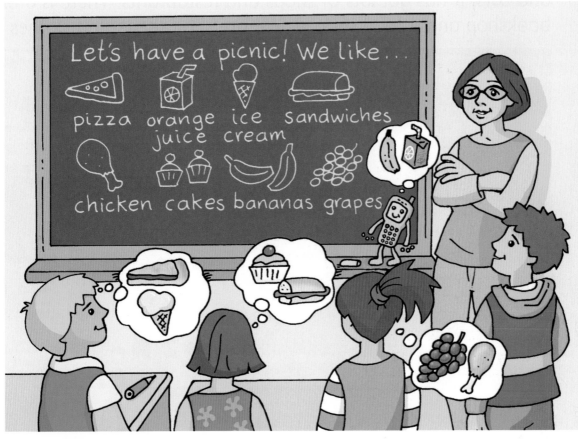

1 **Look and write.**

The children love picnics. Tilly likes _____

_____

_____

_____

_____

Don't forget to draw and write what **you** like, too!

At the airport

The airport is a busy place. There are many planes and buses, taxis and cars. It has got lots of shops and restaurants. There is a big bookshop and a food shop. There are shoe shops and clothes shops.

I'm Mr Black. I'm a pilot. I can fly planes. My plane is black and silver. My hat is black and silver, too.

I'm Mr Blue. I'm a bus driver. This is my blue bus. It's nice but it can't go very fast. I'm taking people to the plane.

I'm Miss Green and my dress is green! I'm checking the tickets. There are lots of passengers on this plane.

A lot of people are working here. There are lots of passengers. They're waiting for their planes. They're going all over the world.

 I'm Mr Grey. I'm a cleaner and I'm cleaning windows. This is my bucket. There are 300 cleaners in this airport. It's very clean!

 I'm Mrs Pink and I love pink! Look at my pink shoes and socks! This is my pink van. I'm taking the food to the plane.

 I'm Mr Red and I'm wearing a red jumper. I can carry your bags. Most people have got wheels on their bags. But some bags are very heavy.

Reading and understanding

1 **Read and complete the sentences.**

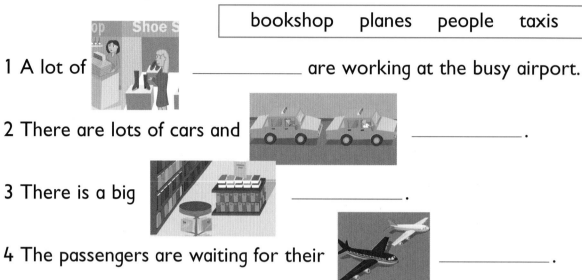

| bookshop | planes | people | taxis |

1 A lot of _____ are working at the busy airport.

2 There are lots of cars and _____.

3 There is a big _____.

4 The passengers are waiting for their _____.

2 **Read and say. Then circle true (T) or false (F).**

1   It is Mr Grey's hat.   T   F

2   They are Mr Black's shorts.   T   F

3   They are Mr Blue's jeans.   T   F

4   They are Miss Green's socks.   T   F

3 **Now point to the pictures, ask and answer.**

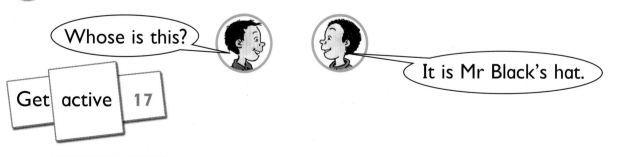

Whose is this?

It is Mr Black's hat.

Get active 17

Working with words

1 **Find the words. Write them in the boxes.**

socks   hat   jumper   skirt   shoes   dress   jeans   shorts   T shirt

j	u	m	p	e	r	a	p
e	y	h	a	t	v	t	d
a	s	h	o	r	t	s	u
n	q	p	i	l	j	h	x
s	o	c	k	s	n	i	w
z	f	r	s	k	i	r	t
d	r	e	s	s	u	t	r
o	g	h	s	h	o	e	s

It is a …

_____ _____ _____

_____ _____

They are …

_____ _____

_____ _____

Sentence building

Words in a **sentence** must be in the correct order.
    I have got socks pink. ✗
    I have got pink socks. ✓

Sentences must make sense.

1 **Correct these sentences.**

1 | I | | ice cream. | | like | _____

2 | I | | can | | planes. | | fly | _____

3 | cars. | | are | | There | | of | | lots | _____

Grammar

Whose hat is this?

It's Tilly's.

Whose socks are these?

They're Sam's.

Remember!

It's = It is   They're = They are

1 **Ask and answer.**

Whose jumper is this?

It's Miss Plum's.

Whose shoes are these?

They're Nina's.

T-shirt   skirt   dress   jumper   jeans   shoes   socks   shorts

2 **Point and say. Then write.**

1 This is Tilly's skirt.   2 These are Ben's socks.

3 _____

4 _____

Listening

Whose voice is this?

1 Listen and number the pictures.

Airport

2 Listen and sing.

Little silver aeroplane
Up in the sky,
Where are you going to,
Flying so high?
Over the mountains,
Over the sea,
Little silver aeroplane,
Please take me.

Phonics

1 **Listen and read.**

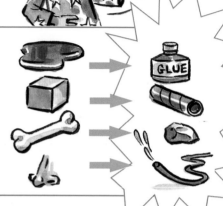

Change **b** to **g** and make b**lue** into g**lue**.

Change **c** to **t** and make **c**ube into **t**ube.

Change **b** to **st** and make **b**one into **st**one.

Change **n** to **h** and make **n**ose into **h**ose.

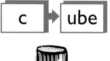

2 **Make the words. Match the words and pictures.**

| bl ▶ ue | gl ▶ ue | c ▶ ube | t ▶ ube |

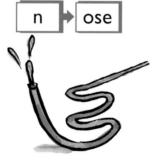

1 _____ 2 _____ 3 _____ 4 _____

3 **Make the words. Match the words and pictures.**

| b ▶ one | st ▶ one | n ▶ ose | h ▶ ose |

1 _____ 2 _____ 3 _____ 4 _____

4 **Tick ✓ the words you can read.**

blue ☐ glue ☐ cube ☐ tube ☐ bone ☐
stone ☐ nose ☐ hose ☐

Phonics focus *words with the spelling pattern* **ue u_e** *or* **o_e**

Class writing

What are the children packing?

shoes   socks   T-shirt   shorts   hat   skirt   dress   jeans

1 **Draw and colour clothes in the bags.**

Nina

Ben

Sam

Tilly

The children are packing. Nina has got _____

_____

_____

_____

_____

Don't forget to write the colours like this:
Sam has got green socks.

Fireworks!

Up in the night sky,
What colour will it be?
When we watch the fireworks,
What will we see?

Mum and I like pink.
My brothers like blue.
Dad likes gold and silver.
What about you?

See the wheel go round, round, round. It makes a whizzing, whizzing, whirring sound.

a firework rose!

Way up high there it goes in the sky,

Blue and yellow,
Pink and white,
I write my name
In the sparkler's light

Bang   bang   crackle   bang

   Parents: *see extra material on page 167*

Slowly, slowly,
It starts to fall.
There's very little
Light at all.

Faster and faster,
On it goes
And now the waterfall
Quickly flows.

A beautiful firework,
A river of light.
It fizzes and falls
And lights up the night.

Watch the roman candle.
See it glow.
Watch the lights
As they go ...

Reading and understanding

1 **Read and match the pictures.**

1 This firework goes round and round. ☐
2 You can write your name with this. ☐
3 It falls slowly, then faster. ☐
4 Way up high. There it goes. It's a firework rose. ☐
5 The candle glows and goes Fffffffft! ☐
6 You can see silver and gold stars. ☐

2 **Read and write the rhyming words from the box.**

go sound white all flows sky

1 fall ———————   2 light ———————   3 goes ———————

4 glow ———————   5 high ———————   6 round ———————

Get active 18

Comprehension focus *consolidation of new language in Fireworks!*

Working with words

1 **Play a game.**

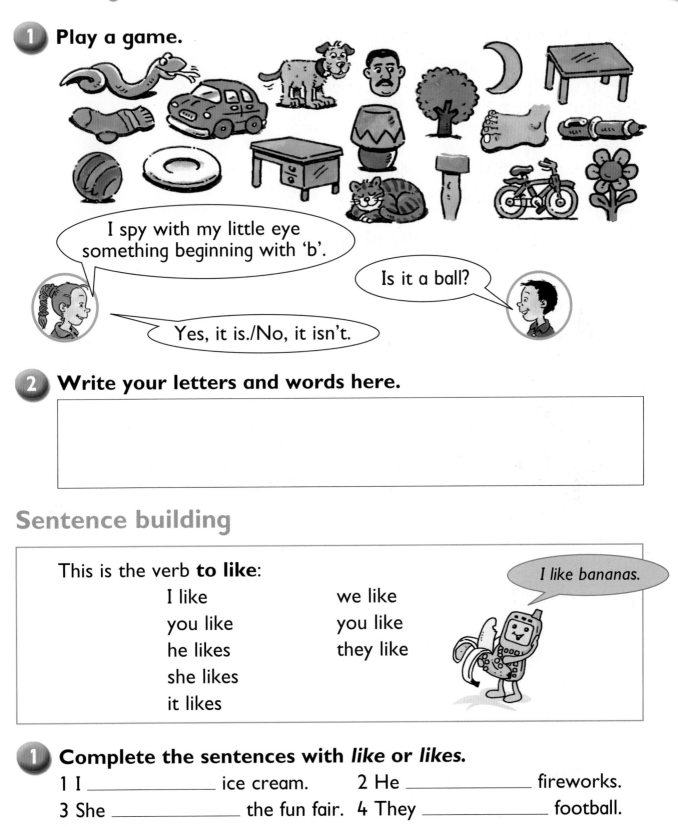

I spy with my little eye something beginning with 'b'.

Is it a ball?

Yes, it is./No, it isn't.

2 **Write your letters and words here.**

Sentence building

This is the verb to like:

I like	we like
you like	you like
he likes	they like
she likes	
it likes	

I like bananas.

1 **Complete the sentences with *like* or *likes*.**

1 I _____ ice cream.   2 He _____ fireworks.

3 She _____ the fun fair.   4 They _____ football.

Grammar

Look at this!

1 **Read and point to the picture.**

The children are walking round the fire.

Miss Plum is throwing a star into the fire.

A firework is flying over the trees.

A firework is flying towards the moon.

Mobi is walking along a branch.

An owl is flying onto a branch.

2 **Say and then write.**

into	onto	over
round	along	towards

1 Ben is jumping _____ the water.

2 Nina and Tilly are running _____ the tree.

3 Sam is jumping _____ the water and _____ the island.

4 Mobi is sailing _____ the river _____ the waterfall.

Listening

What's your favourite?

1 **Listen and write the names.**

Ben   Nina   Sam   Mobi   Tilly   Miss Plum

1

2

3

4

5

BANG   CRACKLE   BANG

6

2 **Listen and sing.**

Up goes a rocket!
Whooooosh! Bang!
Look at all the stars shining in the sky!
Up goes a rocket!
Whooooosh! Bang!
And all the stars fall down.

Listening focus *descriptions with colour and movement*

Phonics

1 **Listen and read.**

My be**lt** is o**ld**.
My mi**lk** is co**ld**.
Can you he**lp** me look for go**ld**?

2 **Find and circle the words.**

1
a b x o l d z q

2
h j c o l d f n

3
k p g o l d q r

4
q b e l t w r t

5
z x c v h e l p

6
b k m i l k g h

3 **Write.**

1
The car is _____ .

2
Sam is _____ .

3
This is _____ .

4
_____ is white.

5
This is a _____ .

6
Sam can _____ .

4 **Tick** ✓ **the words you can read.**

gold ☐   cold ☐   old ☐   belt ☐   help ☐   milk ☐

Class writing

Let's write about having fun!

1 **Look at the picture of the fun fair. Point, ask and answer.**

What can you see?

What is it doing?

At the fun fair.

2 **Now write about the fun fair.**

We can have fun at the fun fair. I can see a

It is going

| Remember! |
| It **is** going.　She **is** going.　They **are** going. |

Revision 6
You can do it!

1 **Look at the pictures.**
Do you like picnics? What can you eat on a picnic? What can you drink?

2 **Listen and read.**

3 **Read and say.**
Look at picture 1.
Who can you see?
Who has got blue shoes?
What have they got on their backs? What is Ben holding?

Look at picture 2.
Look at the map. Where are they going? Are they going into the trees? Are they going under the bridge?

Look at picture 3.
Who wants to swim? Or play ball? Or eat?

Look at picture 4.
Look at the blue bag.
Whose bag is it? What has she got in her bag?

Look at picture 5.
Look at the green bag.
Whose bag is it? What has he got in his bag?

1 The children are going on a picnic. Sam is wearing green shorts and a brown jumper. Tilly has got a pink dress and a white hat. All the children have got bags.

Let's swim!

Let's play ball!

I'm hungry. Let's eat!

5 Whose bag is this? It is Sam's. He has got chicken and orange juice.

What is in this bag? Grapes and biscuits.

2 They are going along the path, around the trees, over the river, towards a waterfall.

This is a good place for a picnic.

4 Whose bag is this? It is Nina's. She has got cakes and a banana.

What is in this bag? Sandwiches and an apple.

6 Look at Mobi! What has he got? Whose cake is this? It is Nina's. Whose sandwiches are these? They are Ben's. Mobi likes picnics.

Mmmm! I like picnics!

Look at picture 6.
What has Mobi got?
Whose biscuits are they?
Whose orange juice is it?
Is Mobi happy?

4 Listen and say which picture. 🎧

5 Act out the story.

6 Listen and say the chant. 🎧

Take a cake from the plate.
Have a glass of cold milk.
Cake and milk. Mmm!
Milk and cake. Mmm!
I like cake and milk. Mmm!

Reading comprehension questions

Unit 1: pages 10-11: *My family and me*

Where is Tim? How old is he? How old is his big brother? Is his dad tall or short? (Repeat this with mum, sister, little brother, grandma, grandpa).

Point to Tim's friends. How many girls are there? How many boys? Point to Tim's teacher. Is it a man or a woman? Who is Jack?

Unit 2: pages 18-19: *A new room for Amy*

Who has got a baby sister? What colour is Amy's new room?/(your room?) Is your bed big or little? Is there a desk (chair, table, etc.) in your room?

Who has got a computer/radio? What colour is it? What is in your toy box?

Unit 3: pages 26-27: *Can the moon see me?*

Point to the moon/sea. What colour is it? Make the shape of the moon/sound of the sea.
Point to the owl. Where is it? What colour is it? What does it say?

Unit 4: pages 36-37: *My secret garden*

Who has got a garden? Where is the nest? What is in it? What is yellow/beautiful? What is black/big/in the pond? Who has got a pond? What colour is the fish?

Unit 5: pages 44-45: *Where is my house?*

Point to house number three. Is it next to number 4? Is it next to number 2? Point to the tree. Point to the house. What number is it? Where is the pink/blue house? Point to number 2, etc.

Unit 6: pages 52-53: *We love the beach*

Where are they? What colour is the sky/sea? What has Mum/Dad/Mikey got? What can Pat see? What has Grandma (Grandpa/Mum/the man) got? What can Grandma hear? What can Grandpa see?

Unit 7: pages 62-63: *Do or don't?*

Where are you in the morning? What can you see? What does Mum say? Point to the bus driver. What does he say? Where are the children? The teacher says ...; The children say ...; Point to the swimming pool. The man says ...

Point to the picture. Can you jump? Can you jump high? Now, where are they? (at home, in the garden/house). Who is this? (Mum, Dad, Grandma, Grandpa) Dad/Mum/Grandma/Grandpa says...
Who likes biscuits? What can you see at night? Dad says...

Unit 8: pages 70-71: *Where are the animals?*

Can you see the owl? What colour is it? Where is it? What is it doing? (Repeat with butterflies, tiger, snake). Which animal can run very fast?

What is in the river? Can you see it? What colour is it? What is it doing? What is walking in the trees? What colour is it? What does it look like? What is white in the picture? Can you see the fox/bear? What is it doing?

Unit 9: pages 78-79: *Playtime*

Where are these children? Are they having fun? Point to the picture. Who are singing and dancing? Who are playing football? Who are marching? Who are climbing? Who are riding horses? Who are skipping?

Unit 10: pages 88-89: *Suki's day*

When is Suki sleepy? When is Suki happy (a bit sad, thirsty, hungry)? What time is it? Do you like milk (pizza, cake)?

Look at the poem. Where is the boy? What time is it? Is he sleepy/tired/sad/happy? What can he do?

Unit 11: pages 96-97: *Here comes the train!*

Point to the train. What is it doing? What can you hear? Name things that are noisy. What are the people doing? Point to them. What is the girl eating? What is the woman drinking? What can you do on a train?

What is the man doing? Where is the train? What can you hear? At the station what is the train doing? What are the people doing? Why?

Unit 12: pages 104-105: *We all love the mall*

Point to the cake shop. What can you see/smell in a cake shop? Point to the bookshop. What is it called? Point to Gino's Place. What can you eat there? How many bike shops are there? What can you buy at this shop? What has the toy shop got? Is it big?

Point to the shoe shop. Who can buy shoes there? What can you buy/see there? How many computer shops are there? Have you got a computer? What can you buy in the supermarket/the clothes shop/sweet shop? What is your favourite shop?

Unit 13: pages 114-115: *Dani can count!*

Where is Sami? What is Sami doing? Who is Dani? Where are the sheep? Can Dani count? What comes after seven/thirteen?

What is Dani doing now? (counting, sitting down, etc.) What comes after thirty/forty/fifty?

Unit 14: pages 122-123: *Splish, splash, splosh*

What day is it? Point to Mum/Sue/Sally. What are they doing? What goes 'Woooooooooo'? What is Susan doing? What's the sound of splashing? What is black? What can Susan hear? What's the sound of thunder?
Why does Mum say 'Oh no!'? What's the weather like? What's the sound of rain? What's the sound of lightning? Who is scared? Where are they now? Where are they going? Is Sally happy? Why?

Unit 15: pages 130-131: *Animal puzzles*

Can you show me (mime) long arms/tails /ears/neck/nose; big mouth/ears/eyes; short legs/long legs? Who can swim? What can swim/fly/eat leaves?

Point to the monkey/rabbits, etc. What have they got? Point to the funny animals (bottom right). What have they got? Point to the child with an owl's head and elephant's feet, etc.

Unit 16: pages 140-141: *Let's have a picnic*

Who likes picnics? Where/when can you have a picnic? Have you got a picnic basket at home? What do you put in it?
Can you point to /Who likes apples/grapes /biscuits/ cakes/sandwiches/orange juice?

Unit 17: pages 148-149: *At the airport*

Why is the airport busy? What shops has it got? What are people doing at the airport? How can passengers travel? Point to Mr Black. What is he? What can he do? What colour is his hat/plane. (Repeat with Mr Blue/Miss Green.)

Point to Mr Grey. What is he? What is he doing? What is the airport like? Point to Mrs Pink. What's her favourite colour? What has she got? What is she doing? Point to Mr Red. What colour is his jumper? What can he do? What is he doing?

Unit 18: pages 156-157: *Fireworks!*

What is the Catherine wheel doing? What can you hear? What can you see way up high? Point to the sparkler. What colours can you see? Point to the waterfall. What's it like? What can you see/hear?

Point to the roman candle. What can you see/hear? What colours are fireworks? Who likes the pink/blue/ silver and gold ones? What are your favourite fireworks? Point to the bangers. How many are there? What can you hear?

Macmillan Education
4 Crinan Street
London N1 9XW
A division of Macmillan Publishers Limited

Companies and representatives throughout the world

ISBN 978-1-405-01367-3

Original design by Oliver Design and Wild Apple Design Ltd
Page make-up by Cambridge Publishing Management Limited
Illustrated by Carlos Avalone, Barking Dog Art, Juliet Breese, Pauline Hazelwood, Shiny Leung, Mike Spoor, David Till, Bill Toop and Gary Wing
Original cover design by Oliver Design
Cover design by Andrew Magee Design Ltd
Cover photographs by Getty Images/Michał Krakowiak, Thinkstock/iStock/AmbientIdeas

The publishers would like to thank the following:
Cambridge Publishing Management Limited

The authors and publishers would like to thank the following for permission to reproduce their photographs:
Alamy/B&C Alexander p72, Alamy/bobo pp20(ball), 23(e), Alamy/Luca DiCecco p37(nest), Alamy/Filmfoto p53, Alamy/FLPA p158(d), Alamy/B.Geduldig p41(frog, mouse), Alamy/Images of Africa Photobank p135(4), Alamy/Juniors Bildarchiv GmbH p41(dogs), Alamy/L.Mason p103(4), Alamy/ Geoffrey Morgan p41(elephant), Alamy/Neilson Photography p57(g), Alamy/S.Sarkis p57(f), Alamy/Steve Bloom Images p41(monkeys), Alamy/STOCKFOLIO p158(e), Alamy/Aleksandr Ugorenkov pp20(plane), 23(f), Alamy/Robert M. Vera p37(pond), Alamy/Tony Watson p158(f), Alamy/Maximilian Weinzierl p37(beetle), Alamy/Zee p52, **Corbis**/Dave G. Houser p37(flowers), Corbis/Peter Johnson p57(d), Corbis/Tom & Dee Ann McCarthy p103(6), Corbis/ Will & Deni McIntyre p57(c), Corbis/Gail Mooney p103(1), Corbis/Pierre Vauthey/ Sygma p23(d), Corbis/Bob Winsett p103(2); **Eye Ubiquitous**/D.Maybury p37(frog), Eye Ubiquitous/M.Powles p135(1, 5), Eye Ubiquitous/P.Seheult p23(a); **FLPA**/S. Hosking p135(2); **Getty Images**/Michael Banks p158(c), Getty Images/John Bracegirdle p135(3), Getty Images/ Comstock Images p23(red plane), Getty Images/Echo p54, Getty Images/John Foxx p57(a), Getty Images/Larry Gatz p103(3), Getty Images/Image Source p158(b), Getty Images/Demetri Otis p28(l), Getty Images/Siede Preis p23(c), Getty Images/Pete Turner p158(a); **NPL**/H.Pearson p57(e), NPL/Anup Shah p103(5); **Photodisc** p41(cats); **Photoshot**/Stephen Dalton p36(butterfly), Photoshot/NHPA pp28(r), 41(snakes); **Rex Features**/C.Bahr p116, Rex Features/Reso p36(apples); **Thinkstock**/iStock/popovaphoto pp88, 89; **Topfoto**/Imageworks p57(b), Topfoto/2004 Topfoto p23(b), Topfoto/Jeff Moore p20(doll), Topfoto/Ria Novosti p36(snake), Topfoto/UPP p20(train).

The authors and publishers are grateful for permission to reprint the following copyright material:
Page 61: *Happy Birthday* words and music by Patty S Hill and Mildred Hall © Summy Birch-Birchard Music, a division of Summy Birchard Inc, USA/EMI Music Publishing, London WC2H 0QY 1935 renewed 1962, reprinted by permission of Warner Chappell Music Ltd.
Page 89: Rose Fyleman: *Sing-Time* from *Fifty-One New Nursery Rhymes* (Doubleday, 1931), © Doubleday, a division of Bantam Doubleday Dell Publishing Group Inc 1931, 1932, reprinted by permission of The Society of Authors as the Literary Representatives of the Estate of Rose Fyleman.
Page 135: Theresa Heine: *Who Is It?* taken from *The Macmillan Treasury of Nursery Rhymes and Poems* by Roger McGough (Macmillan 1998), reprinted by permission of the author.

These materials may contain links for third party websites. We have no control over, and are not responsible for, the contents of such third party websites. Please use care when accessing them.

Printed and bound in Malaysia

2019 2018 2017 2016 2015
18 17 16 15 14 13